ANGER SOLUTIONS

Proven Strategies for Effectively Resolving Anger
and Taking Control of Your Emotions

JULIE A CHRISTIANSEN

Leverage U Press

Contents

High Praise for Anger Solutions!	iii
Acknowledgments	ix
Introduction	xi
1. Wrap Your Head Around Anger	1
2. Step One: Master the Art of Definition	9
Step One Exercise	19
3. Step Two: Know Your Belief Systems	22
Step Two Exercise	33
4. Step Three: Understand How Anger Develops	34
Step Three Exercise	45
Anger Solutions Self-Evaluation Tool	46
5. Step Four: Develop Your Assertiveness Skills	47
Step Four Exercises	60
6. Step Five: Get in Touch with Your Body Language	62
Step Five Exercise	72
7. Step Six: Listen	73
Harmful Listening Behaviours	85
Step Six Exercise	87
8. Step Seven: Release Residual Anger	88
Step Seven Exercises	107
9. Step Eight: Forgive	111
Step Eight Exercise	119
10. Step Nine: Understand the Cyclical Nature of Anger	121

Flying	131
Expand Your Feeling Word Vocabulary!	133
References	139
Also by Julie A Christiansen	141
About the Author	143
Web Presence and Social Media	145
Anger Solutions Success Stories	147
Notes	149

High Praise for Anger Solutions!

"If you are looking for practical tools for expressing anger and finding resolution, Julie's excellent book will gently guide you through the process. In Anger Solutions Julie de-bunks anger myths and sets the record straight about this misunderstood emotion. Learn the truth about anger and how it can be resolved beyond taking a deep breath and counting to ten."
~ Christine Williams
Host of "On the Line", CTS Television
Burlington, Ontario, Canada

"Through her warm, conversational style, Julie clarifies the truth about anger and how our beliefs can affect the way we respond to it."
~ Jacqueline Marcell, Author of Elder Rage!
Host of "Coping with Caregiving", on www.wsradio.com

"Julie is insightful and masterful in untying the often-complex knots of human emotion. Her wisdom and humor are a gift to help us encounter far less speed bumps or conversation collisions and far more clear communication pathways."
~Deborah Charles Wilson,

National Seminar Trainer and Coach
Hartford, CT

"I have read hundreds of self-help books and this one scores at the top - full of meat and potatoes for business and personal relationships - 2 thumbs up!"
~ Reg Goulding
President and CEO, Smile Science Leadership Institute

Leverage U Press, Printed in Canada

Anger Solutions! Proven Strategies for Effectively Resolving Anger and Taking Control of Your Emotions

Copyright © 2003 by Julie Christiansen

Fourth Revision © 2020

Requests for Information should be addressed to:

Leverage U Press

73 Royal Manor Drive

St. Catharines, ON

L2M 4L2

www.angersolution.com

Fourth Revision ISBN: 978-1099946189

All rights reserved. No part of this publication may be reproduced, stored in a retrieval system, or transmitted in any form or by any means – electronic, mechanical, photocopy, recording, or any other – except for brief quotations, without the prior permission of the publisher.

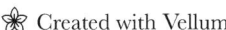 Created with Vellum

This book is lovingly dedicated to my husband Stevan. Thank you for your patience, love, understanding, and your never-ending support. Thank you most of all for periodically reminding me that I am human, and that I must always practice what I preach.

Acknowledgments

Although I cannot name them all, I wish to thank first all those individuals from my parents, siblings, and friends who have contributed to the person I am today.

Thank you to Gloria Grant, my mom and my mentor, a published author in her own right for editing and commenting on the content of this book. Many thanks to my group participants who allowed me to use their stories, and who wrote me letters of thanks and encouragement. To Pauline Fleming, my long-distance coach, thank you for making me accountable and encouraging me to finish what I started.

In the revising of this book, I must thank my tribe: the many Anger Solutions Facilitators, Coaches, Trainers, and Master Trainers that I have had the pleasure to work with over the years; Dr. Mark Ferland, who encouraged and assisted me in developing a standardized measurement tool with which to track our success; and to those who encouraged me to pursue this passion with fervor and to do it with excellence, I offer you my sincere thanks.

I wish to thank those who had the nerve to tell me when I was doing something wrong, and those who challenged me to examine my beliefs. Finally, to my audiences and to those who came to me for counsel and walked with me through this learning process, you have taught me more than I could ever have taught you.

From the bottom of my heart, thank you.

Introduction

There are many common misconceptions about anger: what it is, what it isn't; how it works, why it works; what it's for, and how to express it. Anger is one of those great emotional paradoxes. We as human beings experience anger on a regular basis, but unlike happiness, sadness, and fear, we struggle with its expression. When we're happy we laugh. When we're sad we cry. When we're afraid, we tremble, run, fight, or hide. But when we're angry, we somehow get stuck. Somehow, throughout the course of time, we have come to believe that anger is too volatile, too dangerous, too violent an emotion.

I suppose if you look at the history of mankind, from Cain to Judas to Jack the Ripper to Hitler, the examples we have for coping with anger haven't left us much we can, in good conscience, use. However, there are two sides to every story, and two ways to learn from history. When I think of Joseph, Jesus, Churchill, Gandhi, Mother Theresa, Nelson Mandela, Malcom X, or Martin Luther King, I see another side of anger. I see that anger is different things to different people. What sets one group apart from the other is a little thing called *belief*.

Belief is at the root of everything we do. To borrow from

the title of Dr. Wayne Dyer's books, "you'll see it when you believe it." This is not some hokey, "psychobabblish" notion that is all about "mind over matter". It is a simple truth; one that has existed since the dawn of time yet has been widely ignored or discounted by the populous at large.

When we get up in the morning, swing our legs over the side of our beds, and plant our feet firmly on the floor, we are doing so based on a belief that the floor is still where it was when we went to bed the night before. If we truly believed that while we were sleeping the floor had dissolved and turned into Jello, would we be so quick to jump out of bed? I don't think so.

If you stop to think about it, everything we do in the course of a day is based on certain beliefs we hold to be true. Many of those beliefs are so deeply ingrained that we cannot even consciously acknowledge their existence. If asked to articulate what belief allows us to drive our cars without fear every day; what belief enables us to perform the daily duties of our jobs, or to nurture positive trusting relationships with some people but not others, chances are the majority of us would not be able to articulate them.

The journey of life can and will be virtually impossible to navigate if we fail to use our built-in guidance systems. The most powerful of those is our personal belief system. Beliefs have the power to shape us, to make us, and to break us.

Depending on what you choose to believe in, you may be an incredibly strong individual, with the ability to take on new challenges, to learn new things, to take risks, and to effectively deal with the consequences of your actions. Your choices regarding your beliefs may also transform you into a weak, dependent person, one who is afraid to try, afraid to fail, afraid to succeed, and afraid to take responsibility for your own behaviour.

What you believe about anger is directly correlated to how you respond to situations that cause anger. If in angry situa-

Introduction

tions, you find yourself withdrawing, blaming, aggressing, or retreating, perhaps the beliefs you have held to be true are limiting you and shaping you into a person you do not wish to become.

I suppose that is why I have written this book. There are other books out there that address specific issues like road rage, the anger related to past sexual abuse, anger in marriages, and other similar and valuable topics. All the same, I felt it necessary to look at anger where it begins – at the source, rather than identifying the various triggers that might cause us anger.

If I asked you today, "What makes you angry?" I don't think any of you would have trouble telling me what ticks you off. What if I asked you, "What are the underlying beliefs that cause you to feel angry in certain situations?" Now, there's something to think about.

I was talking with a client about his particular limiting beliefs. I remember sharing with him the notion that belief is the basis of action and watching as revelation dawned in his facial expression. He wrote it down in his notebook in large, bold letters, and repeated the phrase a few times to himself, "Belief is the basis of action." To paraphrase his response, he said to me, "Already, my outlook on life is changing, just by hearing that one statement. I've been paralyzed, and afraid to act; but, if I truly believe that I have something to offer the world, if I truly believe that I am talented, if I truly believe that I am capable, taking steps toward my goals is so much easier! This has been the missing link for me. I wonder why I didn't see it before."

I gave him the same homework that you will be doing later on as you progress through the steps in this book. I suggested that he go home and list everything that he absolutely believes to be true. Then, I proposed that he extrapolate from those belief statements and examine the consequences of each belief. Take a look at how this works:

I believe that I have incredible talent that should be shared with the world.

If I believe this to be true, then I will not be afraid to share my talent (to publish my writing, to sing in front of an audience, to display my art…)

I believe that bad things only happen to bad people.

If I believe this is true, then when bad things happen to me, it means that I am bad.

You see, we all have certain beliefs about anger, and those beliefs dictate our actions. Why else would someone who commits an act of road rage store a baseball bat or a gun in their vehicle, unless they believed that at some point in time that they might have to use it? Would you punch someone in the face unless you absolutely believed that it was the right thing to do at the time?

People use violence because they believe it will get them the results they desire. Someone who is "invisible" in society immediately becomes visible when they hold a gun to the head of another human being, or they mow down a bunch of innocent civilians with their vehicle. Organizations with unknown, unheard of, un-championed causes immediately become newsworthy when they bomb a building, or demand ransom for hostages. They do these things because they believe their actions will get them what they want or need. In the same way, we respond to anger in our own lives with particular actions or words because we believe that those responses are the best way, or the only way, or the most effective way to get our wants or needs met.

My question to you is this: are you sure? Are you so sure that the only way to get respect is to berate and belittle your subordinates? Are you so sure that the only way to get your kids to behave is to beat them? Are you so sure that the only way to get what you want is to make others feel guilty for not knowing and giving it to you before you ask? Are you so sure that the only way to get justice for your cause is to riot, loot, and burn buildings in your community? Are you so sure that squashing your emotions inside of you won't make you sick?

I wrote this book because I have worked with countless people who have struggled with these very questions. Their core beliefs were breaking them, and inherently they knew it but didn't know what to do to change. In every case that I can remember, the underlying issue was the same. The foundational beliefs on which my clients based their behaviour were skewed, faulty, based on something other than reality.

The things we are taught can affect beliefs, just as much as the things we are not taught. Foundational beliefs can be influenced by our life experiences and the value we place on them. The things we see on TV and hear on the radio can affect beliefs. Traumatic events and their outcomes can also influence beliefs.

Conversely, as we grow and mature, those same foundational beliefs affect the way we receive or reject teaching. They determine how we respond to our life experiences, and whether or not we accept or reject the ideas foisted on us by the media. My point is that just because we have always believed that a certain behaviour is right doesn't make it so.

There is nothing wrong with challenging your beliefs; that is, as long as you are doing so in a systematic and open way. Often people will challenge their foundational beliefs by espousing the exact opposite of the principles they have always lived by.

A woman who has remained passive in an abusive relationship one day comes to the realization that she enables her abuser by being passive. She swings to the other side of the pendulum and murders her abusive spouse in his sleep.

A mother that traditionally vents her anger by crying in the bathroom decides that this technique is no longer useful for her. She begins yelling at her children.

Children that have striven for perfection in order to be

accepted, decide it isn't worth the effort. They slack off in school, listen to dark, depressing music and begin using drugs.

A quiet, non-confrontational, community-minded store-owner shoots the robber of his store with a shotgun after being robbed five times.

You see, just because you realize that the thing you have always believed is wrong doesn't make your next choice of belief or action right. Often what is required is not a dramatic 180-degree turn, but rather a slight shift of attitudes, beliefs, and actions.

Anger Solutions provides you with the tools you need to make those subtle shifts, and to challenge your beliefs openly and systematically. The tools contained in this little toolkit will enable you to picture anger for what it really is. They will help you to examine your belief systems and to understand both the positive and negative ramifications of holding on to those beliefs. You will gain an increased awareness of your own responses to anger, and insight into the responses of those around you. Anger Solutions will show you how to free yourself from the bondage that anger puts you in, and how to make anger work for you instead.

The book is written in "steps" as opposed to "chapters". Each step builds on the one that preceded it. It is much like a skill building exercise. The more practice you have, the better you become at utilizing a skill. However, to obtain mastery of a skill, we must continue to build on it as we would build muscle by increasing the level of weights we work with. So, you will begin with gaining an understanding of anger, and continue through the steps until you come to the final step of seeing anger as a cycle.

I passionately believe that as you work on each step in this book, the insights you discover both about yourself and others will amaze you. I also believe that if you leave your mind and your heart open to the possibilities, you will see that making those shifts in your beliefs and your behaviours will not be as difficult as you thought; in fact, if you stick with me through all nine steps, and make a concerted effort to apply each new principle to your life, you will emerge with a whole new level of skill and will reap positive benefits for years to come.

I believe in this material. It has helped me in ways I cannot begin to number, and it continues to help me, because let's face it, I'm human and vulnerable and make mistakes. Sometimes I forget to think before I act. Sometimes I say things I'll regret later. Sometimes I bottle my anger up inside and make myself sick. Then, I will start going through my "stuff" to get ready for a seminar or a workshop, and I realize I haven't been practicing what I preach.

It doesn't take long for me to be reminded of what works and why it works. Sleepless nights, bad dreams, stomach problems, digestive problems, headaches, stress, poor concentration… they all fade into the background when I do what I know is right, and I act in accordance with my core beliefs. I wish this kind of security for all of you who read this book. Read on, then. I'll be with you every step of the way.

Julie Christiansen

1

Wrap Your Head Around Anger

"We cannot go back and make a new start, but we can start now to make a new ending."
~ Franklin Covey

Jim steps silently out of his office at the end of the day. He closes the door gently but firmly, nods farewell to his colleagues and steps out to his car. Stopping at his favourite watering hole, he hands the bartender his keys and asks for his usual drink with the order, "Keep 'em coming."

After an argument with her partner, Susan retreats into the bathroom, locking the door behind her. She runs a hot, foamy bath and muffles her sobs as water fills the tub.

Bob has a short fuse. It doesn't take much to set him off. He screeches his way through traffic, cursing every red light, every bad driver, every delay that stands between him and a smooth ride to the office.

Jim, Susan, and Bob are all angry. How do we know it? What is anger anyway? What isn't it? How is it possible that all of the aforementioned persons are angry people?

If we look at Bob, the fellow with the short fuse, right away we say, "Of course he is angry. Look at what he is *doing*: he is cursing, driving recklessly, yelling at the traffic…" What we just described is Bob's behaviour, not how he is feeling.

If we examine Sue's behaviour, we assume that she is depressed, maybe grieving, perhaps she is just in pain and needs to soak in the tub.

Then there is Jim. Simple observation reveals nothing at all. He is just a regular guy, stopping for a drink before going home at the end of the day. How then do we reach the conclusion that he is angry?

Anger is not behaviour. It is an emotion. It is not something we do or can necessarily see; it is something we feel. Jim, Sue, and Bob all experience varied intensities of anger; however, their behaviours represent their own particular style of expressing their anger.

A common mistake is to assume that only those who engage in road rage or air rage are angry people; only those who go "postal" in their workplace are the ones with anger problems. Not so. The truth is that every human being under the sun experiences varying intensities of anger from time to time. Somehow, we have come to believe that since anger is best identified through behaviour, that anger is behaviour.

The past several years has proved that anger is a stable, enduring part of the human construct, and no amount of anger management tactics will make it go away. What we have also seen in the light of worldwide Black Lives Matter protests, political supporters rioting, storming and vandalizing public buildings, unprovoked assaults, school shootings, hate crimes, and an outpouring of vitriolic abuse on social media platforms, is an apparent inability of people to manage big emotions like anger. Emotions need to be felt and acknowledged. Once acknowledged, they need to be expressed, not managed or controlled. Once expressed, the problems that ignited those emotions must be addressed, and if possible, resolved.

I realize that there are many problems in this world that cannot be easily solved, if at all. There are too many opposing views, too much greed, too many conflicting political agendas, too many narcissists, too many powerful corporations who have no concern for the greater good.

I can't change those things. It is unlikely that you can either. What you and I can do is learn to recognize and acknowledge our big feelings and express them in ways that are safe and appropriate, ways that help us to get our needs met without causing harm to others. That is why I wrote this book.

Why bother?

Of all the human emotions, anger is probably the most misunderstood. Why is it important to understand anger at all? The answer to that question lies in your decision to read this book.

You need to understand yourself. I'll venture that the reason you decided to pick up this book and read it has something to do with your desire to finally do something about the way you currently deal with your anger. Perhaps you are sick and tired of feeling angry and not having any way to express it. Maybe you no longer want to hold it all inside. You're sick and tired of feeling sick and tired, and you are fed up with being everybody's doormat.

Maybe the anger inside you is starting to build, and you're afraid that if it explodes, you may do something you'll regret later. It could be that your relationships are suffering because you tend to act out your anger more aggressively. You don't know why you blow up so quickly or why certain things make you mad. You just know you're ready to change and you need some help. You need to understand what anger really is, how it develops, and why you feel the way you feel! This book will help you to accomplish all of that and more.

You need help understanding others. Perhaps you live with an "angry" person, or you know someone who does. Maybe your biggest need right now is to better understand your loved one who has anger problems. Maybe your difficult person is someone with whom you work, a boss, a colleague, or an employee. You like your job, but you don't like the tension that exists in the office. You're looking for a new perspective – some tools to help you break the ice and help you at least work comfortably together.

You're not sure what you believe about anger. Many of our beliefs about anger are based on our personal experiences or what we learned from television and the movies. The way we were punished as children often affects our ideas about anger as well. In the early pages of this book, your traditional beliefs about anger will be challenged, and you will find yourself gaining new insight about what anger truly is. What you believe determines how you behave. If you better understand what anger is, your beliefs about anger and how you express it will undoubtedly change.

Your self-esteem is in the toilet. When anger is expressed inappropriately, people react. Their reactions are bound to affect those expressing their anger. What if you have been expressing your anger in a way that makes people withdraw from relationships with you, thereby causing you to feel guilty, ashamed, or embarrassed? What if people are avoiding you or treating you in a way that makes you feel small or unloved? What if you are using anger as a way to feel powerful, unique, or heard?

Perhaps you are struggling with guilt because of the things you have said or done in the heat of anger. Garnering a better understanding of anger and how it develops has helped my clients in this particular boat to change their behaviour. When they began expressing themselves in less destructive ways, they found themselves able to recover some of those lost relationships and to rebuild some of what was broken down. A bonus of this result is a decrease in guilt and an increase in self-esteem. Perhaps through exploring new ways to express your anger, you will experience the same results of those who have walked this road before.

Defining Anger

Anger is a part of the human construct. It is a basic emotion, just as much as happiness, sadness, or fear. Anger is an emotional response to an undesirable stimulus. It is not behaviour.

Think of how anger works in terms of a chain of events. First you experience a stimulus or a "trigger", which you define as undesirable. You associate a meaning to the stimulus and decide how to feel. If the stimulus produces the emotion of anger, you will choose how to act. In effect, your belief about an event and what it means for you determines your emotional response. Your corresponding actions will be in keeping with your emotions.

I like the "trigger" analogy because it creates an instant mental picture. Consider what happens when someone pulls a trigger, fully expecting the gun to fire. In a western movie, when they pan in close to the villain's finger on the trigger, and the scene is moving in virtual slow motion, what happens to you, the viewer? Your body responds to the tension of the moment. You might clench your fists, sit on the edge of your seat (preparing for fight or flight), your heart may be pounding, you are most likely putting yourself in the mindset of the victim or the recipient of the gunshot wound, and your mind is racing. You are thinking for the intended victim. "Where can I go, what should I do? Should I attack, should I run away?" What happens then when the trigger is pulled and all you hear is, "click"? What is the feeling you immediately experience? Relief? Hope? Maybe even triumph!

We all have triggers, don't we? Certain objects or smells; sounds or statements; even the way people look at us can set us off and make us angry. The interesting thing to note is that many of our triggers exist on a subconscious level. We are not aware of them, nor are we always aware that they are the link between our emotions and our behaviour. Often times, someone will press one of our "hot buttons" or tamper with our triggers, and we will feel our levels of frustration building as we try to come to terms with the physiological, psychological, and emotional effects of our experience.

Now, you must also understand that the brain is much like a complex computer. It operates based on the programming we put into it. If we neglect to consciously program our brains with appropriate and safe methods for responding to anger, our brains will automatically revert to its "default" setting.

The kicker is that we do a lot of subconscious programming, which often determines our default settings. For example, have you ever said to yourself, "If my mother says that to me one more time, I'm gonna…" or, "The next time my boss yells at me I'm gonna quit!" Those anticipatory remarks are indicative of your default settings.

Did you know that the scenes we watch on television or the big screen contribute to our subconscious programming? The situations we view may or may not be within our frame of reference. If we have been in a similar situation before, we will either agree or disagree with the methods used (by the ACTORS) to resolve the problem. Even if we do not have a frame of reference for fictitious situations –we will make certain assumptions (based on the actors' behaviours) about what is right or wrong to do if we ever find ourselves in a similar situation in real life.

Our default settings can also be a result of what we have

done in the past. Those responses might not necessarily work, nor bring us much satisfaction; but it's what we know, so it's what we do. Too many times, we tend to fall back on those patterns of behaviour we have used in the past to deal with our frustration and anger.

Unfortunately, what we know or what we do are not necessarily what works or what is best. However, it is a pattern or cycle that most human beings settle into, all the while experiencing additional frustration over the unsatisfactory results of their responses to their triggers!

This all sounds quite disheartening. If this is how anger works, how can we ever break out of it? First, we must understand that triggers have a purpose. Recognize that the undesirable stimulus serves to let us know that something in our lives is unacceptable. When the emotional response is anger, we experience one of two basic kinds of anger: righteous anger or selfish anger.

RIGHTEOUS AND SELFISH *Anger*

Righteous anger is the kind of anger that motivates its owner to change the environment. It is the kind of anger that repulses at the sight of injustice in society, unfairness in the workplace, or famine and starvation in under-developed countries. Selfish anger is a function of what Freud called the ID. Selfish anger says, "What about me? What is in it for me? That was supposed to be for me, about me, done to me, done with me, done by me…" When we indulge in selfish anger, we are nothing but servants to this basic emotion.

In his now famous audio coaching class, *Personal Power*, Anthony Robbins describes four classes of experience. A Class One experience is one that feels good, is good for you, is good for others and serves the greater good. A Class Two experience is one that doesn't feel good, but is good for you, good for others and serves the greater good. A Class Three experience feels good, but isn't good for you, is not good for others and doesn't serve the greater good. Finally, a Class Four experience does not feel good, isn't good for you, is not good for others, nor does it serve the greater good.

Indulging in selfish anger will be (depending on your style and what motivates you) either a Class Three or Class Four experience. Serving selfish anger does not benefit us as individuals, it does not benefit others, nor does it serve the greater good. Righteous anger, if expressed and resolved appropriately, serves us by motivating us to do "the right thing" not only for ourselves but for others as well. Doesn't that serve the greater good?

How can we be sure we only indulge righteous anger? How do we know if we are serving anger or if it serves us? If anger is our master, and we its slave, how do we reverse the process so that we are the ones in control of our emotions?

Let's begin by reviewing what we know. Anger is an emotional response to events in our lives that we dislike. We know that there are certain triggers that can put us in an "angry mood", and that many of those triggers operate on a subconscious level. We also know that there are two kinds of anger: righteous and selfish.

It is imperative to understand that much of what occurs in our lives on an emotional level happens without our awareness. Our first goal then, is to increase our awareness about what is happening, how it makes us feel, and what we should do about how we feel. This takes us to Step One of the anger resolution process: mastering the art of definition.

2

Step One: Master the Art of Definition

"Pity those who don't feel anything at all."
~ Sarah J. Maas, A Court of Thorns and Roses

Define Your Emotions

I had a friend who defined every emotion she ever experienced by the words, happy, sad, afraid, and upset. She would watch an episode of her favourite television series and when something happened to a character she liked, she would say, "I'm so *happy* this happened to ..." Her response was the same when she bought a pair of shoes at the sale price; she felt *happy*. When she gave birth to her first child, she expressed feeling *so happy*. Conversely, if she went to the store to purchase a sale item and there were none left, she would feel *upset*. She verbalized experiencing the same emotional response when her marriage broke up.

It was incredibly difficult for us to converse about anything on a deeper emotional level because she did not have a base in her vocabulary to support anything but talk of shallow topics. I found it both fascinating and sad that she had such a limited vocabulary with which to express herself. She was completely unaware that her inability to accurately define her feelings was a hindrance to her ability to communicate with others.

Knowing how you feel, and having the ability to accurately express that feeling, is essential. Try this little experiment right now as you are reading. Think back to the happiest moment you have ever experienced in your life. Focus on that moment and place yourself in that gladdened state. Now, sit back and smile as broadly as you can. Now, with that wide, broad, ecstatic grin on your face, say as loudly as you can, "I'm so depressed!" Monitor what happens to your body as you say the words. You will likely feel your facial muscles struggle to convert your smile into a frown. You might find your posture changing as you say the word depressed.

Interesting phenomenon, isn't it? Have you ever noticed that the more you talk about feeling a certain way, the more you feel that way? That is why it is vital that you carefully define the emotion you are experiencing before you express verbally how you are feeling. Think of it this way: there are varying degrees of every emotion we experience. If you looked at happiness as a continuum from say, content to blissful, there would be a plethora of emotional degrees in between.

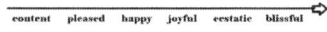
content   pleased   happy   joyful   ecstatic   blissful ➪

Now, if I bought a pair of shoes and got them at 50% off the lowest ticketed price, I might be pretty pleased about that. I most certainly wouldn't be feeling blissful about it. Conversely, if my wedding day was indeed the happiest day of my life, had I expressed my emotional experience as being "just okay" or "content" that would not have nearly begun to accurately depict how I was feeling.

Think about this continuum in terms of anger.

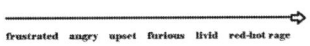
frustrated　angry　upset　furious　livid　red-hot rage

Suppose you are in a busy parking lot during the height of the Christmas shopping season, and you are having difficulty finding a parking spot. Would furious accurately describe your emotion, or would frustrated be a better word?

Now, try that other exercise again. Put yourself in a totally relaxed position, and breathe out the words, "I am so furious!" What happens to your body? Does it tense up? Do your fists tighten? How do those words come out of your mouth? Is your face still relaxed, or are your teeth clenched tight as you say the word furious?

I trust that you can see the power that the words we choose can have over our behavioural responses. It is imperative that we choose our feeling words wisely so that we do not inadvertently escalate mild feelings into intense emotion. As we talk more about this in future chapters, we will examine how knowing exactly how we feel will help us to better express ourselves when we experience anger.

Define Your Anger Style

What is your anger style? When you experience anger do you walk away? Do you drop the gloves without a second thought, ready to hash it out? Or like Sue from the previous chapter, do you run to a private place and cry in secret? The above are all examples of differing styles of anger expression. Out of the following descriptions, see if you can identify your style:

The Bottler: The person who uses this style is like Jim. They will internalize their negative emotions and the triggers that set them off. They can continue for long periods of time, sometimes for an entire lifetime pretending that all is well, and people admire their self-control and even-tempered nature.

The benefits of using this style are huge motivators to continue with the status quo: they maintain the peace in their environment; in the workplace, at home, in their relationships. They are praised by others as being "even keeled" or "mild-tempered".

The downside of using this particular style is that over time, the physical and psychological effects of internalizing negativity without any form of release are devastating. I have counselled individuals who complained of ulcers, irritable bowel syndrome, spastic colon, insomnia, high blood pressure, diabetes, high cholesterol, Chron's disease, MS, heart problems… The list of adverse effects is almost endless.

I remember attending a course on bereavement counselling, and the facilitator asked us, "Where do you feel your grief?" The responses were amazing. People could readily identify the areas of their bodies that were physically affected by the emotional response of grieving.

In my work as a psychotherapist, I have realized that repressed emotional distress has a way of finding the weakest part of your body and residing there, provoking all kinds of often unexplainable physical symptoms that are all too real for the sufferer.

The same is true for anger. Some people will experience migraines, others, ulcers. For some the physical effect will be heart palpitations, for others it will be upset stomach. But eventually, the prolonged, predominant use of this style will manifest itself physically.

The Controlled Blaster: Sue's style of choice, this is the Bottler with a twist. The person using the controlled blast might use it as a temporary measure, for example in the workplace. Knowing it is not appropriate to take out her anger on her superiors, she might do well to hold it in until she can blow "where it is safe".

Like the Bottler, the Blaster can internalize anger for extended periods of time, until the final straw falls upon the camel's back – then chaos strikes. The interesting thing about the controlled blast response is that once the blast occurs, there is a release of pressure both emotionally and physically.

As a result, the physical effects of using this style might not prove as detrimental as those experienced by the individual who favours bottling. However, there are other side effects, which make this choice less desirable. The recipient of the blast, when it occurs, may or may not be the reason for the anger. In any case, allowing anger to build up to a crescendo then exploding is an unhealthy way to deal with issues.

The blast allows for a release of negative energy and provides the user an opportunity to vent; however, it does not speak to the specific underlying issues that caused the blast in the first place. Nor does it allow the user to address the issues that trigger anger with a hope to resolution.

The Chronic Venter: I know someone well who utilizes this style (I'm looking at myself in the mirror…). In fact, many of the mothers I have either counselled or trained, admit that when at home with the kids they use this style.

We have all heard it before: "Why can't you kids keep your room clean?"

"I'm so tired and I've had a bad day, and all I want is a little peace and quiet…"

Perhaps this is the mode of conduct for the office environment – you know, the water cooler talk, "…and then she said this, and he said that…" The venter's style is effective because everyone within earshot knows that the user is upset about something. The problem is, nobody knows what that something is, and after listening to the continual venting, nobody cares!

The Iceberg: Everyone knows at least one person who has used the iceberg at least once in his or her life. Typical situation is this: John upsets Sue, only the poor sod doesn't know it yet. Sue is expertly maintaining her ice-cold front while John tries to figure out what is wrong. "What's wrong, honey?" "Nothing," she responds as she recoils from his touch. She walks away, avoiding eye contact, saying nothing. She mutters to herself, "If he doesn't know what he did by now, well I'm not going to tell him!"

Well, now John knows Sue is upset, but after all, if he makes a couple of genuine attempts to talk it out and she keeps saying nothing is wrong, what choice does he have but to believe her? So off he goes to watch Monday Night Football, and Sue is left alone to stew. Of course, now she is really furious, because he didn't persist as long as she would have liked!

It's a funny mind game if you're watching it on a sitcom, but not so amusing if you have to live it. The benefit of this style is that one can express one's anger silently, without direct confrontation. It feels safe. The negative effect of this style is that no resolution can be achieved because the issue at hand is never discussed. Typically, both parties wait until the storm blows over, or until someone who has been bottling, blasts.

The Scrapper: Ever hear the saying, "We hurt the ones we love the most"? I truly despise that little quote. All too often though, it happens to be true.

Sheila the Shrew comes home after a hard day on the assembly line and slams the door on her way in. She trips over the cat that is leisurely catching a snooze in the afternoon sun streaming through the window. In less than five seconds, poor Fluffy is transformed from sleeping kitty into a screeching projectile as she is booted from her resting place. The babysitter is next, then the kids.

Bob the Beater takes his anger out on his wife because she is too weak, or too strong to fight back. Using an abusive style makes the user feel temporarily powerful, and power is like a drug. When you are in charge even for a moment, the world becomes your oyster. Physical and verbal aggression or violence are vehicles for achieving that desired high.

The downside is obvious: unhealthy relationships (if any), overwhelming guilt, frightened children, unstable, crumbling marriages. And still, the issues that trigger the anger remain unresolved.

The ACME Poster Child: I grew up watching Looney Tunes™ and Merrie Melodies™ on television. Somehow, it was always comical watching Wylie Coyote blow himself up during his futile attempts to catch the Road Runner. He never was very smart – always buying the most unstable dynamite. The truth is that T.N.T. is unstable at the best of times!

The ACME Poster Child experiences anger and responds quickly in an explosive fashion. The ACME dynamite user does not need a particular trigger; everything is a trigger. T.N.T. users live in a state of heightened awareness, always ready to drop the gloves and go a couple of rounds. A consummate Class Four experience, this style is in no way beneficial to the user or the recipients.

Life with a dynamite user is unpredictable, frightening and oft unbearable. The ACME Poster Child has tremendous physical control but has traded it for their lack of emotional control. Bad trade.

Conductor: Don't you love those drum-playing bunnies? They just keep going, and going... This is the secret of the conductor.

The conductor uses the negative energy of anger to power another activity. For example, someone who has had a particularly bad day at the office might go to the gym and work out before heading home. Then they arrives at home feeling less pressured and more relaxed. One might use that negative workplace energy to push ahead with a project that needs to be completed, or to take on extra work. Others might use arts and crafts as their outlet.

At first this sounds like the healthiest of all styles so far; however, there is one caveat I must extend here. If this cathartic expressive style is used without appropriate and effective verbal expression of anger, it can be dangerous.

Think of alcoholics, addicts, people with anorexia, bulimia, workaholics, those who self-abuse… they are all taking the negative energy of anger and using it for another activity; however, the activities they choose are equally if not more destructive. It is altogether appropriate to utilize the conductor style, but in conjunction with appropriate styles of anger expression and resolution. Otherwise, being a conductor will only cause you to become more enslaved to your anger.

Did you recognize yourself in any of the above examples? It is likely that you did. It is also highly probable that you realize that you use more than one of the above styles depending on who you are with, and the nature of your emotional response. This is true for all, but we tend to have one predominant style, which is like the default setting in our brain; it is the one we will go to first.

Why is it so important to know your own anger style? First, knowing your style, its triggers, and the situations in which you typically use them, will increase your ability to curb the use of that style in "unsafe" situations. An unsafe situation is any situation that puts you or others in emotional or physical jeopardy. Knowing your style will make you aware of what you need to change. Furthermore, having an awareness of the different styles of anger will help you to understand the behavioural responses of others, enabling you to respond to them with increased empathy.

Define Your Anger

What kind of anger do you most frequently experience: righteous anger or selfish anger? How can you tell if your anger is justified or if you are acting out of self-interest?

Start by asking yourself some questions and be honest about the answers. This process is called self-evaluation.

1. Is my anger justified? Why?
2. Is anyone else hurting besides me?
3. Why am I experiencing this hurt?
4. Try to examine the situation from both sides as if you were an outsider. Can you see the "big picture"?
5. How do you feel like reacting (what behaviour do you wish to use to respond)?
6. Why would you follow through on your choice of action?
7. If you do what you WANT to do in response to your anger, what class of experience would it be? Would it be a class one, two, three or four experience? If it is a class three or four, you know your anger is selfish, OR that you need to examine some alternative options. If your response immediately falls under a class one or two experience, you will know that your anger is righteous, and you are on the right track.

It is paramount that when you are so angry that you

cannot see straight and you cannot evaluate yourself objectively, that you seek out the ear of someone you trust.

In the next 'step', we will examine the process of self-evaluation and its value in more detail. For now, a picture should be forming in your mind about how self-evaluation can "keep you honest". You should also be growing more aware of the ways self-evaluation can play a valuable role in your decision-making processes.

Step One Exercise

Here are some exercises to help you master the art of definition.

Defining Feelings:

Get a notepad and paper. Brainstorm all the feeling words you can think of. Categorize them into "good" feelings and "bad" feelings. What feelings would you do anything to avoid? What feelings would you give anything to obtain?

Why did you choose these particular feeling words? Make a list of reasons why.

Go to your thesaurus and find synonyms and antonyms for each of the words you chose. Write those down as well.

This week, dip into your newly broadened dictionary of feeling words, and use new words to describe the way you feel about things. Make sure the words you choose accurately describe how you feel.

Defining Your Anger Style:

What is Your Anger Style? Answer YES or NO to each of the following questions.

1. Do you suffer from migraines, ulcers, high blood pressure, diabetes, or some other stress-related health issues? [A YES to this response may indicate that you use the Bottler style of anger expression.]

2. When people rub you the wrong way with inconsiderate of obnoxious behaviour, do you make comments under your breath or keep resentment to yourself [If you answered YES, this response is indicative of the Bottler anger style.]

3. Do you find yourself thinking about how you might resolve a problem in a roundabout way, without the other parties knowing that you were involved? [This is more indicative of a Passive-Aggressive style]

4. When frustrations build up, do you lose your temper or fly off the handle? [If you said YES, you are identifying with the Controlled Blaster anger style.]

5. When tension and aggravation reach too high a level, do you tend to take out your frustrations on someone else? [A YES response indicates the Scrapper style].

6. Do you blow up in a flash, and then cool off just as quickly? [A YES response to this question is indicative of the ACME anger style.]

7. Does your anger build until you explode? [If you answered YES, this means you lean towards to Controlled Blaster style.]

7. When you are feeling angry do you talk to everyone and anyone who will listen? [A yes response is indicative of the Chronic Venter.]

8. Do you tend to avoid the person with whom you are feeling angry, or shut down emotionally and verbally, even if you know you are right? [A positive response would indicate the Iceberg Anger Style.]

9. When you are angry, do you feel the need to have control over your environment by being the loudest person in the argument, or by intimidating others into seeing/doing

things your way? [This would be indicative of the Scrapper style.]

10. Do feelings of anger give you added energy to get work done? [A positive response would indicate the Conductor Style.]

3

Step Two: Know Your Belief Systems

*"The question should never be who is right,
but what is right."*
~ *Glen Gardner"*

Someone once said, "Belief is the basis of action." I believe this to be true. In fact, I passionately believe that the beliefs to which we ascribe directly determine the behaviours we choose.

In my first year of university, I took the requisite, Introduction to Psychology course. Near the end of this first-year psychology course, I remember studying a process called, "scripting". Loosely defined, scripting is performed by the memory and planning centers of the brain to catalogue our experiences and our reactions to those experiences. Our memories of those experiences serve as a basis for how we might handle a similar one if it would arise in the future. Back then, I didn't really care about "scripts" because it was my first year of school, the course was almost over, I already had an A+, and I was having more fun goofing off with my friends.

It took me some time to put the theory of scripting together with many other fine psychological theories, to come up with something that made sense for other than the final exam. I came to the understanding that if our brain works to code our memories and experiences so that we can call on them for future reference; *and* if we can actually subconsciously predetermine a course of action for any number of potential future situations (based on past experience), then belief really is the basis of action.

Most behavioural theories agree that we learn through experience. The most basic of these theories is the classical conditioning theory, which states that when we experience a stimulus that causes pleasure, we quickly learn to repeat the behaviour to elicit the pleasurable response. Conversely, noxious stimuli will elicit negative responses, and we don't want those, right! So, we learn behaviours that will help us to avoid the noxious stimuli, thus avoiding the negative response. Hence, we learn to associate certain stimuli with our experiences if the stimuli repeatedly occur at the same time as a similar response. For example, if I call to my husband (the stimulus), he will answer (the response). I have come to expect this response from him because of my past experience.

The Operant conditioning theory argues that an organism learns that its behaviours will be followed by a particular consequence. An example of Operant conditioning is this: a baby says "mama" for the first time and receives all kinds of positive attention. The next time she says, "mama", she receives positive attention. Because she likes the attention, she continues to verbalize. She has learned that her behaviour elicits a certain consequence. The grandchildren of these theories have incorporated other variables into the learning process, such as our senses, our beliefs, our values, and our broad range of life experience.

We must understand that we are not simply stimulus-response beings who react to our environment without any thought or consideration. We are beings with the power of choice, and what we believe directly influences the ways in which we react to the stimuli around us. For example, in my seminars, I always open up with an icebreaker or a warm-up. My first warm-up question is this, "Tell us who you are, why you are here, then make a statement about something you believe to be true."

I can usually find out a lot about a person by the response they give about what they believe. If a person says, "I truly believe that if you work hard, and do what is right, things will work out in the end", I know that they are dedicated workers who try to do what is right. I know this because it is a given that people want things to work out! So, in order for things to work out for this person, she will act on her beliefs by working hard and trying to do the right thing.

Try this one: "I believe that the words that you speak have the power to dramatically affect people's lives for the good or for the bad." Wouldn't you conclude from this statement that the speaker values the impact his words have on other people, and is careful about what he says?

A good friend of mine once said, "When push comes to shove, you better know what you believe." This is so true! When you are in the midst of a crisis it is no time to start analyzing your belief systems. When my friend made that statement, a light bulb went on in my head. I realized that I had never really thought about what I believed in my heart of hearts. So, I took his advice, and I made a list. Understanding my beliefs has helped me through many difficult transitions and traumatic and tough situations because I didn't have to wonder what the right thing was to do. I simply acted in accordance with my core beliefs.

Belief as the Basis of Action: A Case Study

I remember watching the biography of John Belushi on television. I was quite fascinated by the rise and fall of someone, whom everyone agreed was remarkably and uniquely talented. Of course, one of the aspects of his life that I found most interesting was his beliefs and how they affected his behaviour.

One of John Belushi's core beliefs was that drugs enhanced his performance on stage and on the screen. Because Belushi believed that drugs enhanced his ability to perform, it didn't matter how many barriers his friends and family placed between him and drugs; he was driven to find a way to obtain and use them. When push came to shove for Belushi, it is no wonder that he turned to drugs to achieve enhancement of his mood rather than seek out the comfort of his friends and his family.

Stanton Peele in his article, "The Human Side of Addiction: What Caused John Belushi's Death?"considers the effect that a negative self-image had on John Belushi's death.

"…a negative self-image is so deep and pervasive that no amount of praise or achievement can allay it. Always living down a negative sense of themselves, they frantically seek experiences, which (they believe) will relieve their pain."

Note that I included the bold words in brackets, above. The belief that drugs will relieve the pain is what drives one to seek out the experience of taking drugs. Not everyone turns to drugs when they are suffering because not everyone believes that drugs are the answer.

Peele further posits that people learn to hate themselves when the people who should have shown them support and respect in their formative years teach them that they are worthless or unlovable. A child who has internalized this message, may spend the rest of his life proving the truth of the faulty belief and experiencing discomfort any time a person or event produces evidence to the contrary.

What does this mean, and how does it relate to our discussion about belief systems and anger? If Peele's theory is correct, and Belushi had learned early in childhood to believe that he was "worthless", that fundamental core belief would have served as the foundation for many others that would build his "system" of beliefs.

I am worthless therefore…

- I cannot succeed (worthless people cannot succeed, at least not on their own)
- I may be a success now, but it won't last – I'm not worthy of it.
- I cannot love myself (how can I love what is worthless?)
- I am not worthy of love (because I am worthless)
- I will never be thin, drug free, or abstinent from alcohol and nicotine (my lack of self-worth prevents me from doing what is necessary to quit my bad habits)
- Death is what I deserve (if I have no worth, I have no reason to live)

Are you beginning to see the insidious nature of negative beliefs and how they can shape our lives? As it was for Belushi, so it is for many members of our society. Low self-worth coupled with faulty core beliefs can send people into a downward spiral of poor coping mechanisms, anger, depression and unfulfilment.

Let us now examine the power of belief to shape our experience and expression of anger. We will start by examining the most common myths that we accept about anger.

Myth No. 1: Anger is behaviour

I know you are likely getting tired of reading this over and over again, but a wise man said, "Repetition is the mother of skill". So, hear this again: Anger is NOT behaviour! Anger is experienced as a negative emotion, one of the basic four emotions that we as humans experience: happy, sad, mad, and afraid. According to Dr. Paul Ekman, these four emotions along with contempt and disgust are universally recognizable, meaning that wherever you go in the world, even if you cannot speak the local language, people can recognize and accurately interpret those emotions when expressed on your face.

Here's the thing when it comes to the emotions that humans experience. We do not *do* happy, or sad or afraid. Why then should we expect to *do* anger? We do not use the term, "I'm getting happy!" on a regular basis, but it is not unusual for one to say, "I'm getting mad at you!"

I have found this myth to be the most widely believed in our society. It is what I call a "foundational" belief, because almost every other myth that exists about anger rests upon this first one. It is imperative that we go right to the heart of the matter and change this foundational belief. Once this myth is busted, the other myths will melt away like the Wicked Witch of the West.

Myth No. 2: Anger is BAD

Well... duh! If anger is a behaviour, then of course it is bad - that goes without saying. If anger equals hitting, yelling, screaming, slamming doors, and all the other behaviours we see as negative, then no wonder we see anger as bad. The truth is, experiencing the emotion of anger in and of itself is not "bad", although the ways we choose to express anger can sometimes be labelled as "bad" or "unacceptable". Let us refuse to approach anger with judgement, hesitation and fear, and finally acknowledge anger is neither good nor bad; it is simply an emotion undeserving of judgement or stigma.

Myth No. 3: Anger should not be expressed

If anger is an emotion, then it follows that we should be free to express our anger as freely as we express our other basic emotions. No one thinks it odd that humans express their happiness, sadness, or fear. Yet the popular belief remains that anger if expressed can only lead to "bad things".

In my seminars I have heard it explained this way, "Anger is dangerous…", "Anger is sinful…", "Showing your anger doesn't help you in the end…" Think about this: unexpressed anger has its repercussions as well. Not expressing anger can hold far more consequences for the angry person in the way of ongoing emotional problems as a result of the unresolved feelings.

We also know that unresolved, unexpressed anger can lead to a wide range of physical problems such as ulcers, high blood pressure, migraines, heart disease and stroke, to name only a few.

Myth No. 4: Anger and aggression are the same things

This is a myth that is propagated and reinforced daily by the media and Hollywood. In the movies or on TV, when people get angry, they almost always resort to violence as a means of resolving their anger. It is most important to remember that anger is an emotion. Aggression is only one of many possible behavioural responses to anger.

Remember the "fight or flight" response we learned about in Psychology 101? When the body reacts to a perceived threat, the body's metabolism rate increases as does heart rate, blood pressure, and breathing. Saliva and mucus dry up, increasing the size of the air passages to the lungs. Surface blood vessels also constrict to reduce bleeding in case of injury. These changes prepare the body to attack or flee. They do NOT tell the individual which path to choose.

Now, note I said, "perceived threat", not a "real one". Our perception is based on our experience, values, and senses. So, if our prior experience tells us that the circumstances that we are facing right now are like another experience that proved threatening, we will immediately respond (remember "scripts"?) first on an emotional, then physiological, then intellectual level. First, our brains interpret our circumstances and register the perceived threat. Then, our physiology will put us in fight or flight so that whatever happens next, the body will be prepared for it. Lastly, we try to decide on a course of action, which will hopefully bring us the results we want (the removal of the threat).

Unlike animals, the choice for humans to attack or flee is not such a simple one. We have higher reasoning abilities, which enable us to determine the best course of action or reaction towards the perceived threat. The physiological response to anger ends at the point of making a choice. Any action taken in response to the heightened physiological effects of fight or flight is solely the responsibility of the person taking the action.

Myth No. 5: *Women and children should not express anger*

Again, this is a belief that is perpetuated by the media. Alternatives to this belief are more recently, more frequently being portrayed in the entertainment industry; however, these alternatives only promote inappropriate expressions of anger such as verbal aggression or violence. Many Hollywood films today are filled with scenes of women and children committing unspeakable acts of violence, using language that would make a soldier blush, and all in the name of justice or rightful retribution. There are few if any vehicles of entertainment that promote safe, appropriate, and effective ways of expressing anger.

Small children are often scolded for expressing their anger (by the way, many times they are only doing what they learned from their parents). How many times do we tell our children that hitting or yelling or stomping away is "bad" without offering alternatives to their behaviour? Little children are concrete thinkers, and they associate their behaviour with the way they feel. If we reprimand them for their behaviour without separating it from their emotion, we ingrain in them the foundational belief that anger is behaviour and that anger is bad.

From an early age, children learn that it is better to repress anger rather than to express it, since expressing anger is typically cause for punishment or admonition from a parent or authority figure. Think of how this foundational belief is supported through the school years.

Let's say Steve and Billy are fighting in the schoolyard. The principal calls them into his office and suspends them both. They are punished for attempting to resolve their anger in an inappropriate way; however, no alternatives are given outside of the customary, "shake hands and say you're sorry."

The principal thinks he is teaching the boys to resolve their differences 'like men' (and what, exactly does that mean?); in fact, the differences still remain – there has been no dialogue, no resolution, and no agreement to disagree. Steve and Billy are still angry at one another; they just know that fighting is out of the question. Worse yet, the beliefs that lay beneath the motivation for the fight will remain intact.

What is the right way for the boys to deal with their anger? They're still not sure. To top things off, they will inevitably face punishment by their parents for getting suspended. The underlying reason for the suspension may not be addressed in a way that the boys can understand.

For women, it has long been an unspoken rule that women keep their anger to themselves. Just as for many years, women could not be aggressive in business, nor could they be "overly sexual", it was not "proper" for women to openly express their anger. One theory purports that people transfer their anger and depression through substance abuse. Given that women are disproportionately diagnosed with depression compared to men, it could be assumed that men choose more overt methods for expressing anger, while women turn anger inward, resulting in depression. Another presented by researchers at the University of California, Los Angeles, suggests that men act out their big feelings while women 'tend and befriend' – in other words, they get together in a klatch and talk it out over cocktails and finger sandwiches.

What I have found is that women in general tend to internalize anger, either using the "chronic venting" method of anger expression -- which is highly ineffective -- or by expressing anger in more passive ways like the "iceberg". Although over the years, women have become more empowered within society, effective and assertive ways of anger expression must still be taught and encouraged for everyone, regardless of their gender.

Myth No. 6: *If I express anger, bad things will happen*

Because the myth that anger is "bad behaviour" is so pervasive, it is easy to believe that the expression of anger will result in horrible, dangerous, or otherwise disastrous outcomes. The truth of the matter is that anger only results in horrible outcomes if you choose methods of expression that are maladaptive, inappropriate, unsafe, or even violent. You have the power to choose how you express your ire.

Which of these myths have you always embraced as reality? With which of these are you already arguing? Sit with these concepts for a while. Consider your own anger style and the behaviours you typically choose to express (or conceal) your anger. Why do you lean towards those particular actions? I'll guess that it is because you believe one or more of these myths to be true, and that belief governs the behaviours you choose. You see belief truly is the basis of action.

Step Two Exercise

Exercise:

Make a list of at least five of your core (foundational) beliefs. You may come up with a longer list, since sometimes we have to sift through all the other beliefs that we hold on to, to get to those foundations they are built on. In a crisis, how will these beliefs help or hinder you? Try working through the problem using this sentence format:

If I believe that bad things only happen to bad people, then when something bad happens to me I will... (feel, think, act).

Are all your beliefs based on reality? Or is it possible that some have been developed out of past experience and negative associations? Perhaps it is time to build a new house starting with a solid foundation of beliefs based in reality, not perception.

4

Step Three: Understand How Anger Develops

*"Two ways to fail: Think without acting,
Act without thinking"*
~ Unknown

How do we get this thing called anger in the first place? Isn't that the question? Understanding how anger develops is instrumental in developing safe, appropriate, and effective ways of expressing it.

Let's look first at some of the common causes or triggers of anger. You are probably thinking, "I already know what my triggers are! It's those crazy drivers, those irritating salespeople, my boss, my whining kids…" Although we tend to think that the visible or audible stimuli in our environment are the causes or triggers for our anger, the truth lies more in the fact that those stimuli cause us to feel an emotion. The emotion that is induced by the stimulus is the actual trigger.

Some of the most common causes of anger are felt emotions such as confusion, frustration, and threat. Let's take a quick look at how these words really contribute to the context of anger resolution and management.

Confusion

Confusion could be caused by over-stimulation or sensory overload. This might take the form of too much noise, too much traffic, too many people talking at once with the stereo blasting and the phone ringing, etc.

Lack of oxygen to the brain may also be a factor contributing to confusion. Believe it or not, poor breathing techniques can contribute to this. We will discuss the value of good breathing later on.

Other contributors to confusion are improper or faulty perceptions. One might misinterpret verbal communication due to poor filtering or faulty perception of physical communication due to poor understanding of non-verbal cues.

Misinterpretation of verbal and/or physical communication could also be due to cognitive deficit (developmental delay, brain injury, or other impairment).

Frustration

Consider this example of how frustration translates into anger.

> *I want my voice to be heard. I feel like no one is listening. My desire is not being fulfilled; therefore, I feel frustrated. I want to attract attention, but no one is noticing. I feel more frustrated... My frustration goes unanswered... I feel anger...*

I once had a dream that clearly reinforces this concept. *In my dream, I was desperately trying to dial 911 to report a severe beating of a woman outside my house. The first difficulty was that I had no dial tone due to someone else being connected to my line. I could not convince this person to hang up so I could connect with 911, nor could I communicate effectively how dire the need was that we get an ambulance. In the background, the noise level was mounting.*

Since I could not convince the other party to get off my line, I asked them to get hold of 911 services for me. They agreed, but when I had finally completed giving them instructions to my house and I asked them if they had received all the information, there was no one there!

As you can imagine my level of panic and frustration was mounting steadily as was the volume of noise in the background. Finally, in my dream, my state of anxiety continued to increase until I "blasted", and what a blast it was! I awoke with a start and had a bit of trouble getting back to sleep afterward.

The process of mounting frustration and panic that took place in my dream is typical of what happens in our everyday lives, although not necessarily to such an overwhelming degree of intensity. "Frustration" happens when your desired goals appear to be unattainable. Anger happens when "frustration" begins to build into an emotional crescendo.

Threat

How does threat translate into anger? Remember Psychology 101 and "fight or flight". We are supposed to be beings with higher cognitive functioning and advanced reasoning abilities. However, our advanced reasoning abilities often get us into trouble in that we tend to over-analyze.

More often than not, we analyze the wrong things. Fight or flight is a physiological response that kicks in automatically when something triggers a thought in our brain that indicates a threatening situation. What we must understand is that the threat does not have to be real in order for us to flip into fight or flight mode. A perceived threat evokes the same physiological response as a real one.

Now we must ask, what constitutes threat in a current society? Entering a new work environment isn't threatening, is it? How about a junior sales staff pitching a sales proposal or an innovative concept to a skeptical crowd? If you were in that situation might you feel threatened? Some people might perceive criticism as threatening. Others view people of a certain gender, ethnicity, sexual orientation, or religion as threatening.

It is true that in some situations like the aforementioned may, at times constitute a real threat, but again the key word is *perception*. Anais Nin says, "We do not see things as they are, we see them as we are." Our perception of our surroundings and our circumstances too often determines our world.

How Anger Develops: A Choice Theory Model

William Glasser, the founder of Choice Theory describes it something like this… the *real* world is what truly exists inside and outside of our environments. Each individual filters the real world through their senses, past experience and values. Once the real world passes through an individual's perceptual filters, this becomes their *perceived* world or, the world as they see it. Every individual also has a mental picture of how things would be, could be or should be for them to be happy. This is the *ideal* world or the *quality* world. Frustration is what results when the perceived world and the ideal world don't match up.

Example: In the real world, my employer tells me I should take more initiative in my job. My past experiences with negative criticism, compounded by my belief that even constructive criticism means I am not doing everything right, cause me to perceive my boss as challenging my ability to do my job. In my ideal world, no one would ever criticize my actions. The lack of congruence between my perceived world and my ideal world sends a frustration signal to my brain. In this case the frustration signal manifests itself in the form of anger (defensiveness) – "I take plenty initiative around here. If he thinks he can find somebody better to do the job, I dare him to try!"

Frustration (according to Glasser) is what motivates an individual to act. Several theories agree on this point. You must be dissatisfied enough with a situation before you make the move towards change. Frustration is defined in Choice

Theory as any stimulus that causes you "pain" (physical, psychological, or emotional).

It follows then, if anger is manifestation of the frustration, and the anger is not resolved, individuals can respond in one of two ways. They can turn the anger inward or outward.

How Anger Turns

Anger turned inward

Think of the "bottler" style of anger expression. The effects of this style are generally physiological in nature, as the angry person is usually the only one who knows they are angry. Some examples of somatic responses to this style are ulcers, headaches, colon problems, eating disorders, insomnia, and generalized anxiety. We could say that the act of turning unresolved anger inward is the result of thinking without acting.

Anger turned outward

Imagine the "controlled blaster" or "the ACME poster child". Unresolved anger turned outward can present itself as verbal aggression, verbal abuse, physical aggression and/or physical abuse - or a combination of the above. We could say that the act of turning unresolved anger outward is the result of acting without thinking.

In both cases, there is an obvious lack of balance in these responses and actions. How then does one achieve balance? Glasser says that the individual performing a *self-evaluation* at the point of experiencing the frustration signal will achieve balance.

We have already been conducting exercises in self-evaluation. We have been asking questions of ourselves, taking a closer look at our behaviours, our motives, our beliefs and our feelings. The goal of self-evaluation in an anger situation is to strike a balance of thinking *then* acting.

T.S.A. A Practical Application

Think!

Before you do anything else, think about how you are feeling. Remember, acting before thinking is basically *not thinking*. Outburst control in most cases is selective. This means that most people outburst when they know they will get away with it. Even a split second taken to evaluate a situation and how you are feeling in it may change your anger response.

Say!

Assertiveness is the key to anger resolution. Passivity leads to anger turned inward. Aggressiveness is anger turned outward. Saying how you feel gets it off your chest, so you don't stew. It also opens up an opportunity for you to resolve your anger with another person.

Ask!

Open up a dialogue. The other person may not even know they are contributing to your anger. Dialogue empowers both parties to make a change and to contribute to the process of change.

How many of these skills do you feel you have? Which are you comfortable using now? With which ones do you feel uncomfortable or vulnerable? If you already use some of these skills, do you feel you are using them effectively?

As you ask yourself these questions, you are continuing the process of self-evaluation. Life is a series of questions looking for answers. We tend to go through the process at a subconscious level, which is why we end up getting such crummy answers a lot of the time. By performing conscious self-evaluation, we increase our awareness not only of our surroundings and how they affect us, but also of how our behaviour affects others.

I'm sure you are wondering about how this formula applies to everyday life. Think about how anger translates into behaviours. Remember, not all behaviours are overt demonstrations of what we typically believe anger to be. So, as an example, think of some of the signs of anger in the workplace.

- A busy rumour mill
- Sarcasm
- Faces -- gestures and faces people make when someone disliked walks by
- Not-so-civil disobedience against authority figures
- Passive-aggressive behaviours (manipulation, deliberate forgetfulness, willful ignorance)
- Lateness, truancy, abuse of sick days
- Slamming doors, stomping
- Sighing heavily
- Apparent surrender, which is meant to imply "you are an idiot, but I wash my hands of you. When the poop hits the fan, you can take the blame".
- Icy silence
- Withdrawal from social situations
- Veiled threats
- Overt threats, verbal/physical aggression, or abuse.

When you think about each of these examples, do you recognize anyone you know? Perhaps even yourself? Think about how the T.S.A. formula might eliminate or decrease some of the behaviours or activities listed above.

To take the formula of T.S.A. a step further, let's break it down in terms of self-evaluation.

Think

A participant in one of my facilitator boot camps gave an example of a man with antisocial personality disorder. When someone made this man angry, his immediate response was, "I wanna kill the guy!" It didn't seem to matter how you reasoned with this individual, he only wanted to "kill the guy".

Given the nature of this man's diagnosis, it is not surprising that "kill the guy" was his default response. Most of us, however, do not choose to kill first then ask questions. It is most preferable to ask questions first, like:

- What just happened?
- What does it mean?
- How do I feel about what just happened?
- What is my desired outcome? How would I like this to work out?
- What am I going to do about it? What are my options for responding?
- What might happen if I choose this option? What is the best thing that could happen? What is the worst thing that could happen?

This process may take only a few seconds, or it may take several minutes, even hours before you decide how to act. Isn't it better than defaulting to "kill the guy"?

Say

We haven't talked about it much until now, but I am finally going to introduce the "A" word: Assertiveness. Once we decide we are going to assertively address the issue that is causing us anger, here are some tips as to what *not* to say:

- "What's your problem?"
- "I think you've been dropped on your head once too many times."
- "You are such an idiot!"
- "Get away from me!"
- "I wanna kill ya!"

No, these types of statements will not get us too far down

the road of anger resolution. The key to *saying* something is in being assertive. Assertiveness means that you voice your opinions, feelings, desires and needs truthfully and compassionately, without intentionally hurting, violating, or belittling another person.

Have you ever heard the saying, "My rights end where yours begin"? This wise statement surely applies to the art of assertiveness. It is best to use statements which speak to how you feel about the situation rather than what the other person did to *make* you angry.

An example of using "I" statements is this: "I feel (emotion) because you (behaviour)." There is your first assertive statement. You must be very clear about how this particular behaviour affected you. This is why it is so important that you have a good vocabulary of feeling words to choose from. (See the Appendix for a list of "feeling" words you may be able to incorporate into your vocabulary.) You must be able to accurately describe to a person how their behaviour affects you emotionally.

The second statement is one that indicates what you would like to see happen or what you would have preferred to happen. It can be as simple as asking that the behaviour not happen again, or you could give examples of how your particular situation or circumstance might have been handled differently. For example, in the case of mishandled office politics, you might say, "Perhaps if you had come to me with your concerns before going to the supervisor, we would have been able to avoid this misunderstanding. From now on, if you are ever bothered by something I've done, please come to me first."

Now, if you are feeling angry and are not sure why, it is perfectly acceptable and even preferable to indicate that you are feeling angry, but unsure of the cause. Your next statement would then be to indicate that there is not much sense in talking about it now, but you would like some time to think about what has occurred, and then discuss it later when you are not so emotionally charged.

Ask

Now that you have started something, you must be prepared to finish. You can't say, "You're a big jerk!" then run away. This is not appropriate nor is it an effective technique for anger resolution. Once you open up a dialogue, you must allow the other party to have their say.

After you have made your "I" statement, and given your perspective, the next thing to do is to ask the other party to give some input. "Do you understand where I'm coming from?" sometimes works. (Once I tried that and the response I got was "no". I honestly thought I had done a good job of expressing myself too!) "What is your perspective on this?" or "How do you feel about what I just said?" sounds rather clinical, but both questions are appropriate and effective. The best option is to ask for input on what can be done differently to avoid frustration anger arising repeatedly over the same issue in future.

Again, you cannot and must not ask for some input then walk away once the person starts to talk! If you start the dialogue, see it through. Remember that if you expect people to hear you out, you must extend the same courtesy to them. Hear them out, and if you disagree, then so be it! At least you are talking about it now, and even if all that comes of the dialogue is that you agree to disagree, you will still have come a long way from feeling hurt or angry.

Last but not least, you must understand that T.S.A. is not a "one shot deal". As you are engaged in dialogue, the other party may say something with which you disagree! When that frustration signal strikes, begin the process again. Think about it, and then decide what you will do or say. Be sure your decision is safe (both for you and all other interested parties), appropriate, and as effective as it can be.

Follow through with the formula and repeat it until you

have some closure, or until you agree to disagree. If you are in a situation where confrontation is not possible, express your feelings to someone you trust, then use the conductor style to release the negative energy. Be sure to tap that energy into a positive task!

Step Three Exercise

Exercise:

Here is a short list of questions that will aid you in the task of self-evaluation. This list can be used over and over again, whenever you find yourself in situations in which you are experiencing anger. Try to determine which "world" (real, perceived, or ideal) each question addresses.

Anger Solutions Self-Evaluation Tool

1. What is happening in this moment/What just
2. happened?
3. What does this mean? What value or meaning am I assigning to this event?
4. How am I feeling in this moment/How was I feeling when it happened?
5. The way I want this situation to be resolved (my ideal resolution or outcome) is:
6. What can I do to achieve my desired outcome for this problem? (List all possible options).
7. What is the worst thing that could happen if I choose each of the options listed above?
8. What is the BEST thing that could happen if I choose each of the options listed above?
9. What I plan to do to resolve this situation, and why:

Now that you have done a bit of self-evaluation, you have more information with which to make a decision as to how to express your anger safely and effectively and to resolve the situation.

5

Step Four: Develop Your Assertiveness Skills

To be passive is to let others decide for you. To be aggressive is to decide for others. To be assertive is to decide for your self. And to trust that there is enough, that you are enough. ~ Edith Eva Eger

As we have learned in the previous chapters, we all express our anger in some way, either inwardly or outwardly. The most common types of behavioural and verbal expression fall into three categories: aggressive, passive, or assertive. Of course, we cannot forget about those we would consider passive-aggressive.

Before I start defining or describing the three major categories of expression, let's do an "Assertiveness Self-Check".

Assertiveness Self-Check

1. When people treat me poorly, I call it to their attention. Y/N (Assertive)
2. I finish other people's sentences for them. Y/N (Aggressive)
3. I am reluctant to speak up in a discussion or debate

even when I have strong opinions on the subject? Y/N (Passive)
4. If a friend is late returning borrowed money, books, or clothing, I will mention it. Y/N (Assertive)
5. I continue an argument even after the other party has indicated they want to stop. Y/N (Aggressive)
6. I frequently step in and make decisions for others. Y/N (Aggressive)
7. I often give people the silent treatment when I'm angry with them. Y/N (Passive/Aggressive)
8. It is easy for me to refuse unreasonable requests from your friends, colleagues, or acquaintances. Y/N (Assertive)
9. If people have done me wrong, I will work behind the scenes to find a way to "get back at them" for wronging me. (Y/N) (Passive/Aggressive)
10. When I am telling someone a truth that they might find painful, I speak to them with care and compassion. Y/N (Assertive)

How did you rate on these questions? When you were asking yourself these, were you trying to decide in your mind whether your response indicated passivity, aggressiveness, passive-aggression, or assertiveness? Which of these questions if answered "no" or "yes" indicate a high level of assertiveness?

What do you think assertiveness means? We all have pictures in our mind of aggressive people and passive people. (Think, for instance, of Popeye and Olive, or Tarzan and Jane. Perhaps you remember your "strong, silent" grandfather, and your harping grandmother.) What does an assertive person look like? Let's first clarify the various communication styles.

Ways We Express Emotions

Aggressive

The aggressive individual has little or no consideration for the rights and feelings of other people. Aggression can be indirect in the form of gossip, gestures, or sarcasm; or it can be direct in the way of verbal or physical assault, threats, name calling, public humiliation, hostile remarks, yelling or throwing things.

Aggressive people may achieve their goals, but at others' expense. Sure, they are expressing their feelings, but doing so hurts other people in the process. Aggressive people may try to make choices for others. Those around aggressive people may feel taken advantage of, humiliated, abused, or embarrassed.

Aggressive people may often feel self-righteous, justified, superior, and powerful. The intent of aggressive behaviour is to dominate or humiliate. This sounds like a terrible profile to have associated with one's character, right? So why would anyone want to engage in aggressive behaviours? Because there is a payoff!

Remember this, everything a person does, he does for a reason. If we were not meeting at least some of our needs by doing certain behaviours, we would not do them! William Glasser maintains there is no such thing as common sense, because people do what makes sense to them. If being verbally abusive brings the desired results (or makes sense), then why change?

The long-term negative consequences of the behaviour are not as powerful an influence for change as are the immediate consequences (getting what you want and having control). The payoffs for using aggressive behaviour are being able to vent the negative energy of anger while feeling superior, powerful and in control.

Need I describe the negative outcomes of using this style? Why not take a blank piece of paper and write down all the reasons why you think this style would be damaging to an individual who chooses to use it? You can feel free to use the descriptions of the anger styles from Step One to help you.

Passive (Non-assertive)

People with passive communication styles have trouble expressing their wants, needs, ideas, feelings and opinions; or expresses them in a self-depreciating way. We have all heard someone say, "This is probably a stupid question but…" the classic self-deprecating remark. They not only have to deal with the reality of hardly ever getting what they want, but they also must cope with the guilt, anxiety and disappointment of constantly battling between wanting to be heard and being too afraid to speak out.

Sometimes, the passive person feels superior; "keeping the peace" is his way of having significance and power. He could rock the boat if he really wanted to, but he is bigger and better than all of that, right?

The passive person may deny himself or put himself down, does not express his real feelings, often feels hurt and anxious, allows others to choose, and seldom gets what he really wants. The intent of these types of behaviours is to please others. The message this individual sends to the world is, "I'm not okay, but you sure are."

Passive people might rationalize their behaviour by calling the result a Class Two experience: remember, it doesn't feel good, but is good for you, good for others and serves the greater good… But we have to keep in mind that the greater good, must somehow serve us as well. Being passive does not feel good; this is true. Is it good for you?

Ask Sue who has to take her ulcer medication three times a day. Is it good for others? Sure, if the "others" are aggressive types. Everything may look good on the surface, but if the passive person is left with guilt and anxiety, and the "others" can only feel irritation, pity or disgust with his or her lack of spunk, then passive behaviours do not serve others or the greater good.

Again, we ask the question "why?" Why do people use this style? The payoff is that in volatile situations, at least on a superficial level, the peace is maintained. Unpleasant situations, conflicts, overt tension, and confrontations are avoided when the passive approach is utilised.

Passive-Aggressive

The passive-aggressive behavior or communication style is characterized by showing indirect displays of aggression like gossiping, making faces, throwing things, eye-rolling, or using sarcasm.

Passive-aggressive people use manipulative behaviours – e.g. "forgetting" to share important information so the other person looks stupid or negligent; filing complaints about the other person when they have done nothing wrong; making back-handed compliments; setting people up for failure; treating a person nicely to their face while undermining them behind their backs.

This type of behaviour may influence others to feel vengeful, anxious, or confused. Continuing to engage in this communication style will inevitably lead to a lack of trust, suspicion, and poor-quality relationships.

Assertive

Before we get too much deeper into the discussion of assertiveness, allow me to share this story. About two years ago I wrenched my back quite badly after a day of digging up my garden. I was suffering from intense pain, so I booked appointments with both my chiropractor and my massage therapist. The appointment with my massage therapist was first, and he applied heat to my back as he always did prior to torturing me. He then told me to come back the next day.

I went directly from there to my chiropractor who very assertively expressed his displeasure that the massage therapist had applied heat to my back! The heat had swollen my muscles to the point that the chiropractor could not manipulate my spine into its proper position. He commanded me to return the next day, and to let the massage therapist know that he should not apply heat to my back.

Now, the problem was this. My massage therapist was a very outspoken, direct type of guy; outspoken almost to the point of being aggressive in his manner. In fact, he was the type of guy who would greet you by saying, "Go in there and get undressed, okay!" If he didn't like what I was reading while I got my massage, he would remove it without asking and say something like, "You don't wanna read that garbage! Here, I'll show you my pictures of my wife and me in Vegas. Here. Take this brochure home to your husband and tell him he better take you there for your next anniversary. See this ring? Me and my wife got matching ones when we got married again at the little white chapel…"

This fellow, although he was a great therapist, had no bedside manner. He never took "no" for an answer, or that is how it seemed.

The strangest thing happened when my chiropractor advised me that I should confront the massage therapist. I was honestly afraid to do it. The next day, I got up and went to work fighting this incredibly overwhelming anxiety all the way. I even thought about calling the massage therapist to cancel the appointment so I wouldn't have to deal with asking him not to use heat. It was about ten minutes prior to my appointment when I realized that I had to get a grip. Here I was, an assertiveness trainer struggling with exercising my right of consumer choice!

To make a long story short, my anxiety upon entering the massage therapist's office was just about to reach maximum levels. But I decided that pain relief was more important to me than keeping the peace with my massage therapist. So, I very bravely approached him and said, "Uh – my chiropractor says I shouldn't have heat applied to my back before an adjustment, so if you don't mind, could you just adjust me without using the heat pads first?"

Would you believe he patted my shoulder and said, "Good for you! Okay, no heat, just go in and get undressed, okay!" Despite my anxiety, I took the assertive option and won. You see, even after years of practicing AND preaching assertiveness, I still needed a reminder that assertiveness works.

Assertive people express their wants, ideas, needs and feelings in direct and appropriate ways. They are honest, and while they speak their own minds, they do so with the intent to communicate effectively rather than intentionally using their words to harm others.

The assertive person chooses for herself what she wants, and often achieves her goals; she allows others to move toward achieving their goals. She is not intimidated by the progress of others, because she respects herself as much as she respects others. The message she sends is, "I'm okay, and so are you."

Typically, other people like assertive people, because they don't play games, they don't try to intimidate, and they don't try to impose feelings of guilt on you. Their intent is to communicate, not to dominate. They feel confident and good about themselves, and they tend to make others feel respected and valued.

What is the obvious payoff for this type of expression? Well, let's see... other people respect us, we respect ourselves, we often get what we want since we are brave enough to ask, we feel good, other people feel good about us, and when they are around us, we have good relationships, we have improved self-confidence... It would seem that assertive behaviour is the behaviour of choice!

There is one challenge. If assertive behaviour doesn't make as much sense to us as aggressive or passive behaviours do, then it won't be the behaviour we choose! Let's return for a moment to the questions asked at the beginning of this chapter. To which questions did you answer "yes", and to which did you answer "no"? Why do you do the things you do? What is it about that kind of behaviour that makes you repeat it over and over again? How do you feel when you are in the middle of expressing yourself a certain way?

The way you feel when you are using a certain style of expression, or behaviour, is the key to understanding why you continue to use it. Do you feel safe? In control? Protected? Secure? If the reason we act a certain way is that it makes sense to us, you must figure out how your behaviours make sense for you.

If assertive behaviour doesn't make as much sense to us as aggressive or passive behaviors do, then it won't be the behaviour we choose!

Martin Luther King Jr., in a letter written while he was imprisoned in a Birmingham, Alabama jail said this, "Frankly, I have yet to engage in a direct-action campaign that was 'well timed' in the view of those who have not suffered unduly from the disease of segregation." To what was he testifying? That people must experience a high degree of dissatisfaction before they will be motivated to change their circumstances!

If you are not experiencing a high level of unhappiness, frustration or dissatisfaction with your present circumstances or coping methods, you will not be motivated to do anything about them. Glasses describes it as a "frustration signal", that which is the motivation for action. Robbins calls it "leverage". No matter what you call it, it means the same thing – if we are to change our behaviours, we must be motivated enough to do so, and the change we choose must make sense to us.

Think about it. It was after 400 years of slavery that the children of Israel made the move to get out of Egypt. And look at how much convincing it took them to go! It was after over 340 years of oppression and unfair treatment towards blacks that one frustrated student decided she had had enough of racial segregation and refused to sit at the back of the bus reserved for Blacks only. Just how dissatisfied are you with your passive or aggressive behaviours?

We can sometimes experience righteous anger, and still struggle with finding appropriate ways of dealing with it. It happens all the time. People are treated unfairly at work, and they are justified in their anger, but they respond by stirring the rumour mill or by trying to sabotage the person who makes them angry. Someone is deliberately cut off on the highway and decides to respond to his justifiable anger by chasing down the bad driver and beating him with a baseball bat, which was conveniently stored in the trunk.

Just because your anger is righteous does not mean that the response you choose will be. This is why the Bible instructs us to never go to bed angry. This little nugget of wisdom in effect instructs us to address anger before it builds up into something that might cause a blast later. The Bible also instructs us to "speak the truth in love"; loosely translated, be assertive – tell the truth, be honest, but show a caring attitude, especially when you are saying things that might hurt (e.g. sharing criticism).

Practical Application for Supervisors: Offering Criticism Assertively

As a supervisor in the worlds of non-profit, business, and in clinical private practice, I have had to practice "speaking the truth in love" quite often, when giving feedback or doing performance appraisals. There is something inherently anxiety-provoking about performance appraisals to begin with. We always go in a little nervous, and we worry that some silly mistake we didn't know we made will come back to haunt us. Who needs to have a review that is riddled with loads of negative criticism and only spotted with positive feedback?

Many supervisors make the mistake of thinking that the performance review is their opportunity to take their shots at employees for all the mistakes they have made since their last review. Personally, I have never had much respect for a supervisor who cannot speak to an issue immediately; rather the manager waits six months to blindside an unsuspecting employee at their performance review.

Why not offer ongoing feedback? Supervisors could use each informal feedback session as an opportunity to see if their employees have some specific learning or development needs in order for them to do their job more efficiently. Ongoing feedback also allows the supervisor to nip problem areas in the bud rather than letting them go for extended periods of time without any intervention.

The problem in following through with this concept lies in the fact that most people prefer to avoid confrontation. We would rather wait until the six-month or one-year review and get it over with all at once rather than having to continually address problems. However, if we are to be effective as supervisors, and if we expect to get the most out of our employees, ongoing feedback is the way to go. Remember there is a difference between constructive and destructive criticism. Constructive criticism is the only kind that should be flowing from supervisor to employee. Destructive criticism erodes self-esteem and morale and contributes to an unhealthy work environment.

When in a supervisory role, T.S.A. is not the best formula to use, especially when feelings should not have that much influence on what is supposed to be an objective report.

The approach I most appreciate, and the one that I aspire to emulate when giving feedback is this:

Ask. Start by opening up a dialogue. Ask how things are going. If they are experiencing difficulties in any specific areas, what kind of support do they need from you? Some people are totally oblivious to the fact that they are experiencing difficulty or that they require support. In this case, you would want to point out the areas in which you notice they are having trouble. How do we do this while instilling confidence in the employee that we believe they are capable of making the required improvements?

Say. My preferred format for this aspect of the dialogue sounds something like this, "This is what I see, and this is what it means to me." In real life, it might sound like, "These are some of the things that I have observed…they indicate to me that you might be having difficulty in this area." I do not believe that it is a supervisor's role to tear down an employee's self-esteem; I would rather view a supervisory role as mentorship. A mentor is available to teach, assist and support in the learning of new skills.

This does not mean that we do not set boundaries, or work on goals, deadlines, quotas, whatever is necessary to measure improved performance. It might even be necessary to indicate that disciplinary or remedial action might take place in future if the behaviours taking place (or lacking) are having a negative effect on the workplace. The key to making this kind of heavy statement supportively is in our body language and our tone, as much as it is in the words we choose (see the next chapter on Body Language). What happens now that you have given your feedback?

Continue the dialogue. Ask if they can see the merit of the feedback that you have given. What kind of support do they require from you as a supervisor? It might help if you come armed with resource materials that address the problem areas and offer copies of them to the employee. Let them know you are on their side, and you want to see them succeed in their job. If you have struggled with similar challenges in the past, if might prove helpful to share that, and pass on the resources that assisted you in overcoming those challenges. You then become allies, not enemies.

Most of all, *apply your listening skills*. Give lots of opportunities for them to think aloud about the discourse so far, to internalize what they have heard, and to work through any areas of the review that they think are unfair or unfounded. Remember we don't see things as they are, but as *we* are. You must allow for the possibility that you could be wrong about some of your observations due to the way you see things.

I promise you, this method is more effective than the old sandwich method courtesy of Mary Kay Ash: give a little good feedback, fill the sandwich with negative comments, then gloss it over with another slice of "…but, you're a valued staff, so work on these things and everything will be just fine". Proverbs 11:25 says this: "A generous man will prosper; he who refreshes others will himself be refreshed." Think of the awesome opportunity you have as a person in authority to contribute to the lives of those who serve under you! Consider it well. Do you want a reputation as an unfair, overly critical, unhelpful boss, or do you want to be remembered as one who refreshed and encouraged others?

"Making others better is a boomerang".
John L. Mason

I realize that I am digressing from the topic of assertiveness a bit, but I want to drive home the value of this skill within the context of leadership. Without assertiveness, we cannot contribute to others in as meaningful a way as we are capable. Take careful note of these words from John Mason's book, An Enemy Called Average.

We should look for opportunities to invest of ourselves in others and help make them better.

Somebody did that for you once. Somebody saw something in you and reached out to help you. That act of kindness has determined where you are today. It may have been your pastor, your parents, a friend, a teacher, coach, neighbour, or just someone who offered some extra money, prayers, good advice or equipment and supplies. But whoever it was, that indi-

vidual had the foresight and the resources to invest in you and take a risk on your future.

...Take a few minutes and reach out to help someone else get ahead. You will find that this will be one of the most satisfying experiences you've had in a long time.

(John L. Mason, 1990)

Assertiveness is the skill required to approach someone confidently, and to offer help when you know they are struggling. It is having the ability to say without fear or apprehension, "I think, I feel, I want..." How many passive people wish they could help, but are afraid to offer? How many aggressive people can only say, "I want..." when what they really mean is "I need..."? Assertiveness is what enables you to say, "I am struggling, and I need help."

Some of you might not be struggling with this concept, but I know that there are those out there who do not believe that they can be assertive. Think about this: when you ask a salesclerk to help you find an item in a store, you are being assertive. When you hail a cab, you are being assertive. When you initiate looking for work, you are being assertive. When you asked your partner to marry you, you were being assertive! So, don't tell me you don't have it in you to be assertive. Stop thinking of assertively expressing your feelings as a prelude to conflict!

Why not challenge your beliefs about what might happen when you say how you really feel? You can do this by evaluating each situation on a conscious level. Use the self-evaluation tool provided for you in Step Three, and face down the demons inside your head. Assertiveness pays in multiple dividends with higher returns than you could ever imagine. Try it for yourself. Even if your investment is minimal, but it is made with complete sincerity, you will see immediate returns.

Step Four Exercises

Exercises for developing your Assertiveness Skills:

Find an opportunity to use the T.S.A. technique for expressing yourself. You may even want to role-play with a friend or your spouse before trying it out "in the real world". Don't forget the formula!

T:Think – How am I feeling about this situation? What would I like to see happen?

S:Say – I feel … because … I would like it if…

A:Ask – Can we work this out? How do you feel about…? Can you understand how I am feeling? Could we talk about this some more?

Perform a self-evaluation on your utilization of the technique.

What have you learned so far?

How comfortable do you feel using "I feel" statements?

How did you feel during the discourse? How did you feel afterward?

What areas do you need to change in the way you express yourself?

Are you willing to give up the short-term benefits of your

aggressive or passive styles so that you can reap the long-term benefits of assertiveness?

Think of ways that you are already assertive. Write them down in the form of a list. Make sure the items on your list fit the definition of assertiveness provided.

Can you think of areas in your life in which you wish you were more assertive? Do you wish you were more proactive rather than reactive in the way you deal with conflicts? Make a list of these as well.

Now, think of one situation in particular in which you need to be assertive, but have been avoiding it altogether. Perhaps you need to apologize for something you did; maybe you would like to let someone know about a way in which they have wronged you unwittingly. It could be something you want to ask for or express your opinion about. Go through the self-evaluation exercise and ask yourself what is the worst thing that could happen if you express yourself assertively. Now, what is the best thing that could happen? Take the leap! Apply your assertiveness skills to this particular situation that concerns you and document the results. Always look for what you can learn from each experience and document those as well.

6

Step Five: Get in Touch with Your Body Language

Confidence attracts copycats!
~ Aniekee Tochukwu Ezekiel

In one of my group workshops, I asked a participant, "What does your body do when you are faced with a confrontation?" He stared at me blankly, then after some thought replied, "Well, I just try to stay calm, and I wait until the other party is finished…"

"Yes, but what does your body do? What does it do while you are trying to stay calm?" He couldn't answer me. He kept referring back to what was going on in his head, or his rationale for not 'getting angry', but he could not describe in words how his body reacts to his anger. Perhaps I did not phrase the question properly. Maybe I should have asked him, "What does your body do to indicate that you are trying to stay calm?" Can you see where I'm going with this question? Hopefully, your answer is YES. I am talking about body language.

Did you know that as much as 80% of our communication is non-verbal? Non-verbal communication sends an emotional message to the world. This is why we can meet a person who might not speak our language, but we can still communicate through hand gestures, facial expressions, even through touch. We can acknowledge a connection with another person (or lack thereof) without speaking a single word.

I remember once many years ago, my husband and I were having a heated argument. I cannot remember what we were discussing, but I don't think it was that important. I do remember feeling like he wasn't listening to me, and that I felt like withdrawing from the conversation. I was sick of arguing and didn't want to talk anymore. But we were in the car driving home, and I couldn't walk away. Up to this point in time, we had been holding hands. When I decided to withdraw from the conversation, I removed my hand from his.

The act of retracting my hand sent a strong, clear message that I was no longer interested in being involved with our discussion. It also sent another message: "I can't walk away from you now, but if I could, I would."

I remember this incident because that single, simple action had such an impact on the remainder of our ride home. We both fell into an icy silence. I was hurting. I didn't want to fight. I wanted to hold his hand, but I felt I had to make a point; so, I stubbornly refused to relent. He was hurting too, because of the messages I had so clearly sent to him by letting go of his hand. Most of all I remember how it felt to be so lonely even though I was in an enclosed space with the man I love. It is not an experience I have gone out of my way to replicate in our relationship.

Perhaps you can relate to my story. You see, we all communicate non-verbally. Some methods of non-verbal communication are very overt, while others are quite subtle. Let's look at these from the most subtle to the most overt.

How Does Your Body Talk?

Body Posture

Have you noticed how you can tell a lot about people by the way that they carry themselves? What do you immediately think when you see someone who slouches when he walks? When you see someone six feet tall sit down in a chair and he is suddenly shorter than you are?

When I was a teenager, my mother was always telling me, "Stand up straight, correct your posture." But I didn't want to stand up to my full height because inside, I didn't *feel* my full height.

A slumped position can communicate several different things: a feeling of being oppressed, weighted down, lack of confidence, low self-esteem, depression, tiredness, passiveness… Imagine going in to see your boss to request a raise while projecting this type of image.

An overly rigid body position tends to indicate tension. When you see folks walking or standing with every muscle in their body tensed, you immediately start to wonder what is stressing them out. When people clench fists, grit teeth, or physically tense up, they are sending messages with their bodies. What do you think those messages might be?

When you are watching your favourite sport and someone scores a goal, or hits a home run, or gets a touchdown, how do you know that the fans are happy? Are they walking around with eyes downcast, sighing heavily, or are they jumping up and down, applauding exuberantly and cheering wildly?

Think of people you know who exude confidence, with whom it always feels good to spend time, who seem to be pretty 'together'. How do they carry themselves? How do they walk, how do they express their opinions, wants and needs? Watch what they do and emulate their behaviour. Their body language is talking "assertive-speak".

Body position in relation to others/physical distance

Have you ever tried to have a conversation with someone who is standing too close to you? It feels a little uncomfortable doesn't it? What happens when you try to make some distance between you, and the person moves with you? How do you feel? A bit intimidated or threatened perhaps? Personal space varies from individual to individual, but it averages from 18" to 48" depending on the person.

What happens when someone is standing too far away, but is trying to carry on a conversation with you? Do you find yourself wondering if they are afraid of you? Maybe you smell. You might start checking your deodorant to see if it is still working. Maybe *they* smell! Why won't they come closer? Standing an uncomfortable distance apart sends a non-verbal message.

Finally, the way you move your body, either in gradual, fluid movements, or in tight, jerky actions may communicate grace, poise, or discomfort. The way you gesture with your hands, either flashing them about wildly or hanging them limply at your sides will also tell those around you how confident or insecure you are.

Facial Expressions/Eye Contact

Doesn't it just make your day when someone smiles at you? How does it feel when someone is staring at you, and refuses to break eye contact? Frowns, scowls, smiles, raised or furrowed eyebrows, teary eyes and squints all make a statement. The way you frame your mouth or move your lips (pursed, tightened, loosened), may tell the person with whom you are speaking quite a bit about the way you may be feeling.

Tonality

The way in which we speak, the tone of voice, the way we accentuate words, the loudness and speed of our words as well as the clarity and fluidity of our speech all communicate passivity, aggression, passive-aggression, or assertiveness depending on how we use them. Consider a mother asking her child to stop a certain behaviour. She may start by saying, "That's enough, please stop it."

As her frustration builds, she might become more exasperated. Her tone of voice will go up a notch, she might place more accentuation on the word, "stop". Let's say the child continues with the behaviour, and as the mother loses all patience, her words come spitting out something like this, "STOP – THAT – RIGHT – NOW!" The forcefulness with which she tells the child to stop this time commands attention. Why? Because the child knows that now, Mommy is really upset!

Now, consider the big picture. Think of someone that you know who has poor posture. Perhaps this someone is always slouching, sinking down in her chair at meetings, or she never rises to her full height when in the presence of someone who intimidates her. Maybe she has trouble making eye contact. She talks in subdued tones, sometimes covering her mouth with her hands; you get tired of asking her to speak up so you can hear what she is saying.

She doesn't get too close to people when she is in a conversation; perhaps she even avoids social gatherings in which she would have to approach new people and make small talk. Does this person project assertiveness, aggression, or passivity?

How about the fellow who is always tensed up? Everybody comments on how high-strung he is. He is always huffing or complaining about something… He stands too close, talks too loudly, stares at people in a way that makes them want to find a hole and jump in.

He scowls a lot, furrows his brow while drumming his pencil on his desk, perhaps he paces his office impatiently. When he wants something done, he doesn't just ask for it, he demands it with a loud, forceful tone of voice and the reddened face to match. Do you recognize this person as passive, aggressive or assertive?

Let's not forget about those folks who run to social media to spew nasty comments while hiding under the cloak of anonymity, or the people working in offices all over the world who roll their eyes when someone speaks up in a team meeting, 'forget' to pass along important information that you need to get your job done, or who will create chaos in a project, but happily throw others under the bus when the poop hits the fan. Passive-aggressive behaviour and communication appears to be on the rise these days. Back-handed compliments, snide remarks, rude quips made under the breath, exclusion from email threads, and gaslighting – these behaviour choices are clear indicators of passive-aggressive communication.

Of course, we all know that person who seems to have no difficulty expressing her feelings regardless of what they are. She typically operates in a "pleasant" mode, although when she is angry, she will say so. She maintains an appropriate distance when communicating with another person and does not over or under-gesture with her hands. She doesn't fidget or cover her mouth when she speaks.

Her tone of voice is even, and moderate (not too loud, not too soft). When she is asking for something, she makes sufficient eye contact but doesn't overdo it by staring. Does she project the attitude of aggressiveness assertiveness, or passivity?

Surely you can see the differences between the examples provided here. Now let's look at how you fare in recognizing your own body language messages. Below are some scenarios to think about. Place yourself inside each scenario. If necessary, close your eyes and visualize yourself interacting within the scenario as though you were watching a scene in a movie. Pay close attention to the way your body moves, the way your mouth forms, what happens with your eyes, your shoulders, and your hands. Try to document what you observe on paper.

1. You have just received news of a family member's

death. How does your body react to this sad news?
2. You are at a party and see someone you would like to strike up a conversation with. How does your body indicate that you are a friendly person?
3. You are in an argument with a co-worker. She is badgering you to see her point of view and you refuse to budge. What is your body doing?
4. You have had a fight with your spouse/significant other. You know that you were wrong, and you want to apologize. While you are trying to get your apology out, what is your body saying? Is your body also "apologizing", or does your posture, proximity, facial expression and tone of voice continue to communicate that "I am the one who is right"? Are you only apologizing with your mouth? If your body language is in keeping with your apology, what does it look like?

Self Esteem and Body Language

Our levels of self-esteem have a direct correlation with how assertive, passive or aggressive we will be. Even if we are making a concerted effort to make our verbal communication assertive, if self-esteem is low, our body language might sabotage the entire effort. In not-so clinical terms, we might call this, sending "mixed messages".

Body language can get in the way of effective communication if assertive speech is overridden by unfriendly non-verbal communication (looking stern, frowning, rarely smiling, or staring). If we communicate that we are constantly angry through speaking in a 'professional' tone of voice, being too firm, tightening our lips, using a flat, final tone that excludes others' opinions; even if we are speaking very assertively, our vocabulary will be lost on the recipient. The hearer will only remember that we seemed to be quite angry about something. Furthermore, if we rarely make eye contact, speaking too softly, in effect communicating that we are passive, it won't matter how assertively we speak. Our actions always invariably speak louder than our words.

How can a realistic and positive self-esteem help one to become more assertive? Self-esteem is the value you place on yourself, the feelings you have about yourself, the thoughts you have about yourself, and your sense of being a worthy person. It is related to and can affect the way we see ourselves in the world, as well as our belief that we can achieve the goals we set for ourselves.

If we believe that we are valuable, if we like ourselves, if we are confident in our abilities and we feel "worthy" of other's affection and friendship, then it follows that we will portray that confidence and self-assuredness in our communications.

We will not be afraid to ask for things, because we won't feel unworthy of receiving them. If we are confident in our abilities, we won't be afraid of asking for that raise or disagreeing with the boss. If we like ourselves, then we will behave in ways that will reflect that self-liking. We will not allow others to run roughshod over us, nor will we treat others with lack of respect. Having positive self-esteem makes being assertive easy.

How does assertive behaviour increase one's self-esteem? Let's say a passive person is trying to break out of the mold of always using passive forms of communication. She begins by trying to be more assertive in expressing her wants, needs or opinions. Let's say her first few attempts don't work (due to lack of congruence between her verbal and non-verbal communication), but she decides to keep trying.

When she succeeds at using an assertive technique, what will she feel? Relieved, pleased, perhaps even proud! Then, as she experiences the positive emotion of pride in her accomplishments, what happens… her self-esteem rises. Why? Because she feels more valuable, she feels good about herself for achieving this new accomplishment, she thinks that the effort was worth it because she is worth it! She thinks perhaps this goal she has set for herself is attainable, so she continues with the assertive behaviour. As her self-esteem increases, she in turn becomes more and more assertive.

The key to developing assertive body language is to become aware of your present styles of communicating non-verbally. You should have made some notes earlier with regard to how your body behaves when expressing sadness, friendliness, stubbornness, remorse, and fear. Now think of the reasons you have for maintaining those types of behaviors; I'm talking about your thoughts about yourself, the way you value yourself or the way you think others value you. Here are a few examples:

- Unless I raise my voice, no one will take me seriously.
- I must use the ACME style so people will know I can't be bullied.
- I have to establish and maintain eye contact in order to keep someone's attention.
- If I speak too loudly, they will think I am angry.
- If they think I am angry, they won't like me.
- I can't make eye contact, I'm too afraid of him/her.

Having positive self-esteem
makes being assertive easy.

Remember the importance of self-evaluation! Become aware of negative self-talk, then change it to positive self-talk. This will take more than just turning a negative sentence into a positive one. Start by thinking of situations in which your belief about yourself was challenged. For example, if you believe that you have to raise your voice in order to be taken seriously, think of a time when you maintained your position in a discussion without raising your voice.

Think of times when you gave your opinion, and it was actually considered and you didn't have to raise your voice. If you can't think of a time, ask a friend, your siblings, or your mother. Look back in your life for experiences that directly contradict the erroneous belief that you must be either aggressive, passive-aggressive, or passive in order to make your point.

Another way to develop more assertive body language is to coach yourself. Once you have identified the body language messages you wish to change, try practicing using your assertiveness skills in the mirror. *Yes, the mirror!* Watch yourself: practice smiling, using assertive hand movements, and reducing the frown lines. Make eye contact with yourself, and coach yourself through the process of changing your body language.

I have learned that the best way to develop assertive body language habits is to model the behaviour of assertive people. As I have encouraged you before, find a good role model. Think of someone that you admire; someone whose assertiveness is evident both in their verbal and non-verbal behaviour. Pay close attention to how they express themselves, and how they ask for things. Even pay attention to how they say, 'no'. Observe the way they walk, the facial expressions they use, and the manner in which they use their body to enhance their verbal communication.

There is an ancient saying that if we walk with the wise, then we will also become wise. Follow the examples of assertiveness modeled by those who have mastered its techniques. Soon, assertiveness will become a habit you won't even notice anymore. However, you will notice that the significant improvement of your quality of life and relationships.

Step Five Exercise

Exercise:

Can you think of ways in which you contradict your verbal communication with your body language? List some or all that you can think of on a piece of paper. How do you think others perceive you when your body language is out of sync with your verbal communication? Is that the way you want people to perceive you?

What would you like to change about the way you currently express yourself non-verbally? Would you like to be bolder? Less passive? Less threatening? More welcoming?

Imagine yourself 5, 10 or 20 years in the future, still communicating with the same old mixed messages. Do you see your life as fulfilled? How do you envision the quality of your personal, social, emotional and relational life? Is it better, worse or about the same? Is the way you see yourself in the future acceptable to you, or is it worth it to you to try and improve the odds in favour of a better quality of life?

Why is it important that you change your non-verbal communication? List all the reasons you can think of why your body language must match up with your verbal messages.

7

Step Six: Listen

> *The first and last commandments*
> *of good listening are: STOP TALKING!*
> *Nature gave man two ears*
> *but only one tongue,*
> *which is a gentle hint that*
> *we should listen more than we talk!*

Up until now, I have stressed the importance of dialogue in the process of anger resolution, with a focus on what to say and how to say it. Now, I would like to shift the focus of attention to what is heard and understood. In order to truly hear and understand what others are saying, it is essential to develop the art of good listening.

As I mentioned in previous sections, there is no good in starting something that you don't intend to finish. If you begin a dialogue or discussion in an attempt to resolve your anger, you must be committed to seeing it through to some kind of conclusion. It is unfair to everyone involved to say, ask, then walk away when you don't like the answer you receive. The goal is to stay put and listen even when our physiology, our emotions, and our thought processes are all crying out, 'Attack then retreat!'

We know that when we are in a state of heightened awareness, our physiology reacts right alongside our thoughts and emotions. If your heart is racing and adrenaline is rushing while thousands of thoughts flow through your mind, it will be hard to concentrate. Also, remember that when you are experiencing fight or flight, your body restricts the flow of blood to your outer extremities. Breathing also becomes shallow, thus reducing the amount of oxygen available to the brain. This means we have a person in a heightened state of stress, thinking too much but not very clearly.

If you tend to focus on what your body is feeling, and how angry you are, your thoughts will continue to flow in that direction. If you forget to monitor your breathing and do not make a conscious attempt to slow it down, you will perpetuate the cycle by maintaining the low levels of oxygen circulating to your brain.

You may even attempt to go through the process of resolution, but in this state, you will not be able to think clearly enough to follow through and attain the results you desire. This is because neither your body nor your brain will be functioning at optimum levels.

Practical Application: Using Listening to De-escalate Behaviour

I once had a client who had quite a volatile temper. She was not an expert communicator by any means, and had difficulty expressing her feelings in the ways that we would typically expect or be prepared for. This often led to frequent misunderstandings between herself and those who worked with her.

When we decided to explore the root of her many

outbursts, one of the things she repeated was that she didn't like it when she felt like people weren't listening! In her mind, she was making her best effort to communicate, and we were not hearing or understanding what she was saying. This caused her an immense amount of frustration, and she reacted by acting out her anger.

This was a real wake up call for all of us who worked with her. We recognized that we had to beef up our own listening skills. We had certainly been hearing what she was saying, but we had often misunderstood the context or the meaning of what was said. We took the time to study her methods of communication as well as the ways in which she used her body to relay non-verbal messages.

We found that by changing the way we listened to her, we experienced more clarity in understanding her; thus, she experienced less frustration. We also found that by paying closer attention to her body language, we could identify moments when her frustration was building towards an outburst. We could then redirect the conversation before her frustration culminated in a blast. Because we improved our listening skills, and responded to her body language, we were able to see a significant reduction in her outbursts both with us and with other people.

I remember watching a movie in which a psychiatrist was conversing with his patient. She asked him how he did his job, and he responded, "I take the last two words of the client's sentence, and turn it into a question... Like this, 'Your mother?'"

Although this is a somewhat amusing and fictitious anecdote, if that is all there is to listening, then how come we have so many misunderstandings in the world?

Recently, I was listening to an interview with John Gray, author of, *Men are from Mars, Women are from Venus*. He was talking about how women like to dream out loud, but men interpret dreams as requests. For example, a boyfriend and girlfriend may be driving through a ritzy neighbourhood, and she notices a stately home.

She muses, "What a beautiful house! I would love to have a house like that." He immediately thinks, "How does she expect me to buy a house like that for her? I only make $18/hour! I'm not even sure I want to spend the rest of my life with this woman, and she is already telling me what kind of house she wants us to live in!" He heard what she said, but did he really understand?

One of the things we as human beings do exceedingly well, is we assume. We assume we know what a person's body language is telling us, or we ignore body language and listen only to the verbal message. Sometimes all it takes is for us to see something transpire from a distance and we immediately believe we understand what that something means.

Have you ever been cut off on the highway, and immediately muttered, "Stupid woman driver…" or "Must be from one of those countries where they drive however they like…"? Then you drive past to get a closer look (so you can verify your assumption), only to find out that the driver was a man, or your brother-in-law in a rented vehicle, or a student driver just learning… We hold all kinds of unconscious biases, which feed our assumptions, but they are just those – assumptions. They are not necessarily truth.

Listening to your heart

Now, let's talk more about the importance of listening in dialogue. Every day, I am reminded of the necessity of having good listening skills. One of the skills I find extremely valuable is that of listening to your own gut instinct.

A few years ago, I found myself in a situation where I was caught between two sides of an issue. The proponent of one side was quite vocal, and his argument seemed to make sense to me; in fact, I found myself supporting his position. The other side also made perfect sense, and I supported certain points of that argument as well.

In the midst of all of the commotion and confusion, I felt a little tugging somewhere deep inside of me, somewhat like a child who very quietly but persistently tugs on mother's clothing in order to get her attention. Just as we moms too often tend to ignore that consistent little tug, I failed to recognize the importance of paying attention to that tiny twinge of instinct.

Had I taken more notice of what my instincts were trying to communicate to me, I might have asked more pointed questions of both sides and made more of an effort to get a more complete picture of the actual issue. Because of my oversight, it took me a couple of days to figure out where I really stood on the issue, when in fact it should have only taken me a few minutes or a couple of hours at best.

The relevance of this story to listening is this: when we are in the midst of an argument, fight, or debate, we must be able to detach ourselves from our emotions enough so that we can clearly analyze both the issue, and what is being said about it. This means being able to hear what people are actually saying, as well as what your own internal instincts are telling you; seeing and interpreting body language in an effort to substantiate the verbal communication; and reading between the lines.

We must understand that many human beings have difficulty expressing themselves clearly and succinctly. When it comes to discussing our negative feelings, our vulnerabilities, and our insecurities, that difficulty becomes even more pronounced. We tend to trail off our sentences... You know what I mean? And we expect people to know what we mean! What we are saying is that we want people to be able to understand what we have said even though we haven't really said it.

Whenever possible, we should try to make a concerted

effort to be clear about what we are feeling, what we want or expect, and how we intend to see the dialogue through to resolution. Only through clarity can we communicate effectively to those around us.

Imagine what life would be like if you never fully heard or understood what people said to you. If I said to you, "I'm so tired, I need to sit down and take a break", but you heard, "I am so tired of you, why don't you sit down and shut up", what would your reaction towards me be? You would likely react in anger or defensiveness. Then, I would be wondering what I said to set you off. This is an extreme example although not implausible. People with cognitive deficits, developmental delay or even those with audio-perceptual difficulties like central auditory processing disorder may have trouble interpreting everyday conversation.

When you are dealing with someone whom to your knowledge hasn't any such challenge, it is fair to expect that if they misinterpret your verbal communication, it is because: they are not really listening, or you are not being clear in your communication.

Dialogue is a two-way process. It involves both the giving and receiving of communication. It also requires a willingness to do more than receive information; one must interpret, understand and feed back the information received. The information must also be incorporated into the context of the dialogue, as well as the feelings, needs and wants of each party. Giving someone a lecture does not constitute dialogue. The domination of a conversation either verbally or physically by one party or another does not represent fair, two-way communication.

Listen up!

You may be asking why it is so important to have good listening skills in the process of dialogue, and what are these good listening skills anyway? First, we all want to be heard and understood. No one likes to feel as though their opinions are worthless, or that their feelings are insignificant. You call that certain someone when you have a problem because you know that they will really listen to you. What is it about the way that person listens that differentiates them from your boss or the receptionist at work?

Let's take a little time and focus on the specific skills associated with listening. Effective listening involves creating an atmosphere that shows the other person that you are involved and attentive. You can demonstrate this through making eye contact, maintaining a relaxed and open body posture and appropriate physical distance. While the ideal physical manifestations of "good listening" vary somewhat from person to person - and often vary dramatically from culture to culture - we can typically tell if someone is really listening by their eye contact and body language.

In some situations, we might feel more comfortable to communicate with little or no eye contact. This could be interpreted as an attempt to avoid showing our true feelings about what we are hearing, or that we are intimidated by the other person, or even that we have something to hide. In most cases, direct and frequent eye contact leads to a stronger and more effective message that the listener is both hearing and attempting to understand the message being relayed.

⸻

Practical Application: How good a listener are you?

Test your listening skills. Answer the following questions as truthfully as you can, then do some self-evaluation. Do you think you have the characteristics of a good listener? If you needed someone to talk to, would you turn to someone with your caliber of listening skills?

1. Do you put what you are doing aside, ignore distractions and look directly at the person who is talking?
2. Are you sensitive to gestures, voice tone and facial expressions? Does your own body language encourage conversation?
3. Do you find yourself racing ahead to formulate a response before the other person has finished speaking?
4. Do you have difficulty waiting until someone finishes speaking? Do you finish their sentences for them?
5. Do you give people equal floor time? Do you encourage others to talk?
6. Do you give feedback to acknowledge your understanding of what has been said?
7. If you do not understand something, do you ask the speaker to clarify?
8. Is it obvious to the speaker that you respect every person's right to his or her opinion even though you disagree?
9. Do you respond with judgmental statements?

The following formula that I call, FRIEND, may be useful in helping you to use your attending skills more effectively.

Follow what people say with verbal prompts: "I see..." "Tell me more about it…"
Respect people's right to speak and be heard. Resist giving uninvited advice.
Invite people to speak. Create a safe, caring environment in which they are free to share.
Encourage the speaker to discover their own solutions by reflecting on their verbalizations.
Nodding, touching, smiling, making eye contact and sitting or

standing in close proximity (18" personal space): Non-verbal indications that you are paying attention.
Defer judgement, don't give unwanted advice; don't interrupt; don't doodle, distract or fall asleep.

When you incorporate these behaviours into your dialogue, you demonstrate to the other participant(s) that you are willing to be a true FRIEND, to listen without judgment and to hear out the other side of the argument. Even though you may not get exactly what you want in the long run, you will be respected for demonstrating your willingness to listen.

But I want what I want when I want it!

Many of us think that if we show our vulnerability, or if we take a risk in sharing our true feelings, that justifies our wanting a situation to be resolved the way we want it to be resolved. Not so. The reason we share our true feelings is for our own sake, for our well-being. It is really not about the other person at all.

You see, you share your feelings so that the other individual will know what those feelings are. If you don't say something, they may never realize that they have hurt, insulted, compromised, undermined, or damaged you in any way. So, you tell them. Then you explain how that behaviour has affected you personally, so it has some meaning for them.

Search your motives. If you are sharing your heart with the hopes that the hearer will suddenly fall at your feet and apologize, don't hold your breath. Once the ball is in someone else's court, you have no control.

You cannot dictate, legislate or control the behaviour of others. You are responsible for yourself, and your behaviour; and you are responsible for giving others the information they need to make decisions about their behaviour. Outside of that, don't try to manipulate people with your feelings! That's not what you were given them for.

The reason I say this now, within the context of talking

about listening, is that we often enter into a dialogue with preconceived notions about how it will or should turn out. We tell our spouses or ex-spouses how they have hurt us with the expectation that they will bow down and kiss our feet and make it better. We try to mend a broken relationship by saying, "I want you back," and expect the same response. However, true dialogue is a process over which we have no control outside of ourselves.

It is true that "soft answers turn away wrath, but grievous words stir up anger" (Proverbs 15:1), thus indicating that we have some influence over the tone of a conversation. However, we cannot control what comes out of another person's mouth. What we can do is make sure our ears are attuned to what is truly being said, and not what we *want* to hear!

When you say to your ex-partner, "I want you back", you must be equally prepared for a negative response as you are for an affirmative one. Whatever their response is, you must be willing to hear them out, ask questions, inquire about how they feel, and attempt to understand. Showing an unwillingness to listen will certainly not endear you to the heart of an estranged partner or friend.

To resolve larger issues, it will inevitably take more than one simple dialogue with simple statements and equally simple answers. Be prepared to hear, listen to, and understand all that is said. You will be better off regardless of the outcome.

Reading between the lines

One of the finer skills of listening is reading between the lines. As a therapist, I have found this an essential skill to have because, as I have mentioned earlier, human beings seem to experience difficulty clearly expressing their vulnerabilities and insecurities. I find that people tend to make "thought" statements rather than "feeling" statements, expecting the listener to derive the hidden meaning in what was said.

Practical Application: Active Listening

The method I adhere to for sifting through hidden meanings is dubbed, "Demonstrating Understanding". There are four levels of response to an individual's verbal communication:
(1) responding to thoughts
(2) responding to feelings
(3) responding to feelings and thoughts
(4) responding to personal meaning.

Remember before, we talked about giving feedback and demonstrating both verbally and physically that we are listening. Demonstrating Understanding is a simple but effective model for doing just that. The idea is that you echo what an individual says in different words that might more accurately express what it is that they are trying to communicate.

For example, if your girlfriend tells you about an incident that happened at work, and she says, "That woman is so vindictive…" You might *respond to that thought* with, "You think she did this to you on purpose?" She might then affirm your assessment by saying, "Yes! She does this all the time, and it is always directed at me. I'm so tired of the office politics." This is more of a *feeling statement*, to which you could respond, "It sounds like you're feeling really frustrated."

She might come back with, "Frustrated doesn't even begin to describe it. I can't believe this woman does what she does and gets away with it every day." Your response to this statement will want to *reflect both her feelings and her thoughts…* "You are angry because you do not think justice is being served." You might not be surprised then to hear her say, "That's it exactly! It just makes me so furious that she can carry on however she pleases, and the management just ignores her behaviour! If they only followed policy, she would have been fired long ago."

This last statement indicates that the source of her anger is not only the behaviour of the "accused", but also the apparent lack of concern on the part of the management. You might want to clarify this by *asking about the personal meaning*. "It sounds like you're disappointed in the management because they are not playing by the rules. I guess it makes you wonder where you stand at work if people make up the rules as they play the game."

She may well respond, "You've got that right. I go into work every day wondering what's going on, and whether or not I should abide by policy or play her game. What applies for her might not apply for me, and I don't want to lose my job…"

Do you see how this formula works? You must pay attention in order to be able to hear and formulate responses to what another person is saying. People do not typically make statements that start with, "I feel (feeling word) …" They tend to say, "I feel *like*…" then interjecting verb statements or thought statements. What this does is to encourage the speaker to identify and own their feelings, and to acknowledge why it is that they feel that way. Your role as the listener is to clarify and acknowledge, and perhaps even validate the speaker's feelings.

Notice what does not happen in the above conversation! The listener does not say, "I know how that feels, the same thing happened to me…" Nor does he say, "Well, you should just do this!" The listener only feeds back what the speaker said (hence the word feedback). Try this the next time a friend calls you and begins to vent about their hard day at work.

Respond to their thoughts. "You think that…"

Respond to their feelings. "You feel… (use a feeling word)"

Respond to feelings and thoughts. "You feel… (feeling word) because… (use reason for feeling)"

Respond to personal meaning. "You feel… (feeling word) because you… (personal significance)".

Finally, let me leave you with some helpful hints about what NOT to do when attempting to be a good listener.

Harmful Listening Behaviours

EVALUATION RESPONSE:
"You should..." "You are wrong." "You're such a good person", etc. Agreeing, disagreeing, giving your own opinion can be a block to communication, especially if too early in a conversation.

ADVICE GIVING RESPONSE:
"I think you should...", "Why don't you try...", "You'll feel much better if..." Advice is best given at the conclusion of a conversation and generally only when one is asked for it.

ANALYZING RESPONSE:
"The reason you feel that way is..." "Your problem is..." Most people do not want to be told how to feel and would rather volunteer their feelings than to have them exposed and analyzed.

PRYING, QUESTIONING RESPONSE:
"Why, Who, Where, When, How," are responses common to us all. These responses may make the speaker feel on the spot and therefore resist interrogation. At times, however, a questioning response is helpful for clarification. If you must ask any of the W-5 questions, precede them with softeners such as, "By the way," or "Just out of curiosity..."

WARNING:

"You had better…" "If you don't…" "You must…" responses produce resentment, resistance, and rebellion.

LOGICAL, LECTURING RESPONSE:

"Don't you realize…", "The facts are…" "Yes, but…" These kinds of responses can make the other person feel inferior or defensive.

DEVALUATION RESPONSE:

"It's not so bad, other people are worse off than you, you'll get over it". These responses invalidate the feelings of the speaker.

OVERSYMPATHIZING:

"Oh, you poor thing…" "I would have died had that happened to me." Over sympathizers feel overwhelmed by another person's problems and are sometimes immobilized and unable to help.

WITHDRAWING, AVOIDING:

"Don't think about it." "Let's do something to take your mind off it", "I don't really want to hear about it" are not extremely helpful in the beginning of a conversation.

RESCUING RESPONSE:

"I'll take care of it for you," "I'll speak to … for you", removes the responsibility from the person to solve his own problems and makes him dependent on others.

TOPPING RESPONSE:

"That's nothing, you should have seen…" "When that happened to me, I…" These responses shift attention from the person who wants to be listened to and leaves her feeling unimportant.

Step Six Exercise

Locate your spouse, partner, significant other, your child, or call a friend. Ask them for a half hour of their time and tell them you would like to just talk with them. If you are talking with adults, ask them about their childhood, perhaps pinpoint a memory and ask them to tell you about it. Perhaps you could ask your child about his day at school, or what happened at lunchtime. The object of the exercise is to practice the skill of "Demonstrating Understanding". Refer to the four points provided in this chapter.

1. Reflect thought.
2. Reflect feeling.
3. Respond to feeling and thought.
4. Respond to personal meaning.

Once your conversation is over, make some notes to yourself about how you felt while responding to the other's statements. How do you think they felt? How much did you learn about this person that you never knew before? What is the value of taking the time to really listen to what others are saying?

8

Step Seven: Release Residual Anger

She looked at her old life
One more time
Took a deep breath
And whispered,
I will never see you again.
~ shehaus.com

Until now, we have examined the steps necessary to resolve anger in situations that are presumably fresh in our lives. This chapter will focus on releasing residual anger; that is, the negative emotional energy that stays with us long after an issue has been addressed or even resolved.

Have you ever been in a situation in which you felt angry, expressed yourself, and perhaps even were rewarded with an apology or a promise that "it will never happen again"? Have you ever walked away from that situation still feeling the energy of the anger?

If you recall our chapter on body language, you will remember that when we are experiencing fight or flight, our hearts beat faster, our blood pressure is higher, the flow of oxygen is diverted from our extremities to our major organs, etc. Often, resolving an anger-inducing issue is not enough to bring our bodies back to our base line for stress.

If we allow ourselves to remain in a state of heightened awareness, we put our bodies at risk for high blood pressure, high cholesterol, heart problems, and a multitude of other physical ailments; thus, the value of releasing our residual anger.

The Value of Catharsis

Before looking at the following definition, think about what comes to mind when you think of the word catharsis. Catharsis is defined by Oxford Languages as *"the process of releasing, and thereby providing relief from, strong or repressed emotions."* One might think of catharsis in the context of punching a wall, driving a car erratically, primal screaming, grappling, or boxing.

There are, in fact, countless ways to engage catharsis as a way to release residual anger or other uncomfortable emotions. Some less physical ways to apply catharsis include writing in a journal, creative writing, playing a musical instrument, dancing, or stargazing.

All of the aforementioned activities could be seen as effective cathartic tools *when used correctly*.

A Case in Point

Once I had a client whose primary issues were grief and residual anger. She had experienced a great deal of loss in her young life, and she emotionally unprepared for the effects of those losses to her psyche. As part of the grieving process, she experienced anger for the losses, but had never examined the anger nor come to terms with it. Now she understood that she was angry, and she understood *why* she was angry. She simply had no idea what to do about her anger.

Due to the circumstances in my client's life before she came to me, she admitted that her self-esteem was very low. She divulged that she had created for herself a hard exterior, and that she found it difficult to cry. She further admitted that the only time she found herself able to cry was when someone paid her a compliment. She engaged in behaviours that bordered on being self-abusive and frequently found herself entangled in relationships that were either illicit or otherwise unhealthy for her. Clearly, her anger was turning inward, as she had no means for expressing her anger to those who had hurt her.

For this young lady, releasing her residual anger was paramount to her having the ability to move on, and to desist from repeating the negative patterns she was establishing in her life. Once she found and established healthier ways to release the negative energy of residual anger, and she developed communication skills that helped her to express herself more assertively, she was able to make better quality decisions, and to break the habits that were contributing to (rather than decreasing) her pain.

Writing as Therapy

One of the first things I established with my client was that she would begin to write things down. She frequently had vivid dreams, which more often than not held some sort of significance to her. I encouraged her to describe these dreams as fully as she could in writing before she forgot the important details. We would review the dreams together – exploring the manifest content; sometimes, she would draw the images she saw in her dreams, and we discussed the colours, the shapes and the faces. What significance did those colours hold for her? Who did she believe those faces to represent? Much of the anger she felt at her losses was exhibited in her dreams.

This makes sense doesn't it? If we cannot express ourselves consciously, often our subconscious mind works overtime at attempting to show us where our difficulties lie using symbols or imagery (the latent dream content). Even when hurts are not fresh, open, or bleeding wounds, they still exist. Those hurts must find an outlet – dreams are as good a vehicle of expression as any other.

I had my client write about the experiences in which she experienced the initial losses. Many of her hurts were compounded upon by those losses that followed, meaning she had much for which to grieve over a short period of time.

The writing process takes thought, intellectual examination, and the ability to organize events and to effectively describe those events through the written word. This all takes time. Time is what my client desperately needed – to experience each painful event as a single entity, rather than as part of the unmanageable whole.

As she wrote about each event, she was able to grieve for that single occurrence, to put it in perspective, and to let it go. Often, as she wrote she was able to draw conclusions, to see the situation through the eyes of others involved, which she had been unable to do previously.

She also found it easier to release her pain through crying, as she relived the memories both in her mind and on paper. In fact, as she went through the process of describing her life in writing, there was a period of time in which she cried for days. In her words, it was as though she had experienced a "cleansing" of her memories. Those open and festering wounds from her past finally began to heal.

Journal Writing

Writing is one of the most effective therapeutic techniques I am aware of, because it causes us to slow down and consider carefully what is passing through our minds as we write. In my book, *Top Ten Lists to Live By*, I share the top ten reasons to keep a journal. I will share some of them again here for your benefit.

A journal is a window into the past. In my audio program, *Getting Past the Past*, the focus is in leaving the past behind and facing the future *with more optimism, rather than fear based on failed past events. Even so, there are times when it does the heart good to look back at where we have been and to see how we have grown, improved, and developed since then.*

All too often, we forget where we have come from and what we have already been through. We also tend to forget what worked for us in the past, and struggle with how to address the problems we face today.

A written record of our trials and triumphs is a powerful tool against negative programming. Over time, our memories can fade, but a journal keeps them fresh forever.

Writing helps to put thoughts and feelings into perspective. It causes us to stop ruminating about our problems and forces us to begin focusing on possible solutions. You can say things to a journal that you would never say out loud; and if you're careful about where you store it, it will never repeat your confidences.

In a world where it is increasingly easy to lose touch with one's identity, journal writing keeps you aware of whom you really are. That is one of the joys of writing: you can be brutally honest about your thoughts, feelings, hopes, dreams, and nightmares. Your journal will never judge you. It only listens.

Even if you have never kept a journal in your life, it is never too late to start. All it costs is a $1.00 purchase of a lined notebook, and you can start writing. Imagine how much money you could save in psychologist fees!

Express and Release

What you are about to read is not rocket science though it may seem just as difficult (if not more so). This is only because we are inhibited by our own fears of appearing "stupid" if we try something new or outside of our comfort zone.

Often, I am challenged by audience members or clients who contend that the methods for releasing residual anger mentioned here are "elementary", or "beneath the educational levels" of the audience, and other such criticisms. The truth is that the simplest interventions are often the most difficult to implement. "After all, if it is so simple, why didn't I think of it all by myself? Besides, it may be simple, but I'll look silly. And if I don't look silly doing this exercise, I'll feel silly."

Because of this perception, I spend a great deal of time coaching my workshop attendees and seminar participants how to eliminate negative self-talk.

Negative self-talk is one of the greatest barriers to positive assertion, anger resolution, and the elimination of residual anger. I often ask this question of my audiences, "How many of you, when you woke up this morning, couldn't wait to jump out of bed, strip down naked and look at yourself in the full-length mirror?"

Invariably the response is the same. People laugh nervously, grimace, and groan as they think about how gross they look when they wake up in the morning. They can already hear the negative self-talk coming out of their mouths: "Wow, I look awful. I'm going to have to take extra time to make myself look presentable today." We start first thing in the morning and proceed to beat ourselves up all day. If given half a chance, negative self-talk will effectively destroy all our attempts at resolving your anger.

Let's say that you are dealing with a difficult co-worker, and have decided after much self-evaluation and consideration, that you are going to address her. What are some of the processes that might go through your mind if you are not in control of your self-talk? As you prepare your assertive statements, your negative programming might say, "Who do you really think you are? Do you think you can pull this off? She knows you're a pushover – that's why you have so much trouble with her. She's not going to take you seriously…"

Suppose you get that under control. Then, as you are rehearsing your "speech" in front of a mirror, your programming says, "You look like an idiot. That smile is a fake. Don't show so many teeth. Wow! Are you ever stupid for standing here in front of a mirror. You have no guts whatsoever. Otherwise you wouldn't have to practice being assertive!"

You know that is not true, so you counteract all of those negative arguments with positive ones.

Later on, you are walking down the hall towards her cubicle, ready to ask her out for coffee so you both can talk. Suddenly, you have another negative programming attack. Your knees turn to jelly, and you feel like you're going to vomit. The evil voice in your head says, "You're going to choke. You won't follow through. You know you're a wuss. She's going to chew you up and spit you out."

What will you do now? Do you have the wherewithal to continue combating the voices in your head, or will you retreat to the nearest rest room, all the while thanking God you didn't go through with it?

Be honest with yourself. All too often, the latter choice wins out. The long-term result of "chickening out" is resentment and bitterness. It becomes acceptable to feel that the other party is to blame for your unhappiness. If only your antagonist weren't so intimidating, you would have been able to resolve this long ago. Sure, it is comforting to conceptualize and accept this argument in your head; however, it requires that you abdicate responsibility for NOT addressing the issues that bother you.

I can guarantee you that your effectiveness in the workplace will decrease and the degree of stress you experience at work will increase unless you learn to manage your self-talk. In *Getting Past Your Past*, I spend a little more time identifying how negative programming develops in our lives from childhood, and how to overcome it. I also highly recommend the works of Shad Helmstetter, in particular his book, *What to Say when You Talk to Yourself*.

We all talk negatively to ourselves – don't feel guilty about it. Guilt only serves to make you produce more negative self-talk! Do something about it. The joy of programming is that it can be changed, as long as you know the program language. Fortunately for us humans, we are the authors of our own programs.

Negative programming is what makes you feel silly as you are practicing the techniques for releasing residual anger. If and when you ever feel a negative self-talk attack coming on, use this simple technique for deciding what to do next. Weigh out the pros and cons of whatever technique you are practicing.

If for example, you are attempting the pillow-punch technique, and you feel like an idiot doing it, ask yourself: "Which is better, punching the pillow and releasing my anger or letting it simmer inside until my ulcer ruptures?" I don't know about you, but I think the choice becomes quite clear when you look at it that way. Having said that, let us now examine some of the other resources we have available to us to help us release residual anger.

Taming Aggressive Tendencies

Here is what we know for sure about catharsis. Punching a heavy bag, primal screaming, grappling, boxing, or jamming it out on your guitar or your drum set – *none of these tools will be effective if you have not yet identified and attempted to resolve the problem contributing to the emotion.* As a matter of fact, if you only use the behavioural aspect of catharsis without addressing the underlying problem, it simply will become yet another "quick fix" for your feelings.

Remember the 'conductor' anger style you learned about in Step Two? I briefly mentioned negative conductor behaviours, which can be detrimental to your physical and/or mental health. Activities like smoking, drinking, using banned substances, working overtime in order to avoid relational problems at home, self-harming actions, risk taking, or thrill seeking are all what I call negative conductors, behaviours designed to release or provide relief from strong/repressed emotions.

The challenge with these choices is that they may provide *short-term pleasure*, but they contribute to *long-term pain*. Incidentally, that is what makes these types of behaviours difficult to quit – because the pain is deferred we are less inclined to take the steps to deal with the pain fully in an attempt to make more lasting change.

The key to effective conducting is to:

1. address the problem and seek to resolve it.
2. use healthy cathartic tools to expel or release any residual emotional energy.

Moving forward, we will examine physical, behavioural, relational, and emotional ways to apply the conductor style for effective catharsis.

Before I describe the following techniques, there are some precautionary statements I must make. First and foremost, please understand that there is a reason why releasing residual anger is being addressed at this stage in your reading.

Anger resolution is all about working through problems, taking ownership for one's feelings, expressing them, and actively seeking ways to resolve issues. The techniques described hereafter are not meant to take the place of effective anger resolution strategies; rather, they exist as options for releasing the negative energy that may linger in the wake of an anger resolution encounter.

Secondly, in no way, shape or form are these techniques to be interpreted as a sanction to use aggressive behaviours as a way to resolve anger. First of all, we know from previous chapters that aggression may give us a sense of control or power in the short run, but it is highly destructive to relationships in the long run. Therefore, to now say, "go ahead, punch a hole in the wall when you feel angry", would be to directly contradict everything I have written to this point! Do not misconstrue the purpose for these techniques, and please, do not use your need for releasing residual anger as an excuse to behave in an aggressive fashion.

Releasing Aggressive Energy

If aggression is how you typically express anger, the chances of you changing that style completely are fairly slim. We know that one can alter the way one communicates, and that with enough leverage and motivation, one can decrease – even eliminate – harmful, aggressive behaviours. However, the urge to do something physical often remains. If, after going through all the steps of effective anger resolution, you still feel the negative energy and stress of the situation, you may well need to do something physical to bring your base line back down to normal levels. Here are some suggestions for how to accomplish that.

Pillow Punching, Bozo Boxing, Heavy or Speed Bag

I have often advised my clients to visualize the situation in which they have felt angry or the face of the person who has made them angry. Then, while visualizing, they are to take out their aggressive feelings on an inanimate object like a pillow, sandbag toy or a heavy bag. While engaging in the physical activity of punching the bag or pillow, they are to say out loud why they are so angry.

If you are familiar with neurolinguistic programming (made famous by Michael Brooks and Tony Robbins, you will know that there are three major communication styles: visual, kinesthetic and auditory. Typically, in anger resolution, we focus on visual and auditory styles of communication. The kinesthetic aspect of our communication is often neglected because, after all, we are trying to do something OTHER than fight! This exercise enables us to effectively release negative energy through all three communication outlets.

Remember that often our negative programming will jump in and say, "To whom do you think you're talking? Do you realize what how much you look like a moron?" Just be ready to counter that negative self-talk with reminders that as you perform this supposedly silly task, you are lowering your cholesterol, getting set to decrease your heart rate, rid your body of fight-or-flight, and you are preserving your physical and emotional health.

After any of these exercises, it is paramount that you cool down just as you would after a physical workout. This is time that you can take to empty your mind of the negative thoughts, just as you have emptied your body of the negative energy of your anger. Deep breathing and allowing some time for quiet meditation will help you bring a complete balance to this exercise. The cooling down period is imperative for successfully re-attaining your base line for stress.

Physical Exercise

We all know about the benefits of a regular exercise routine; however, we can all attest to having purchased a membership to a gym, and only going twice. Physical exercise is a classic tool of the conductor style of anger release. The most beneficial mode of exercise, according to my clients, is walking. This is because walking is an immediate option, it is free, and doesn't require any special gear or equipment.

Even if you are in a business environment and cannot simply walk out of the office, you can walk the halls, do the stairs, or just head down to the cafeteria for a coffee. The physical activity releases the negative energy, and the act of walking tends to remove you from the stressful or anger-inducing situation.

Other forms of physical activity are equally beneficial: regular aerobic exercise, stretching, cycling, gardening, and jogging all have a wealth of physical health benefits as well as emotional and mental bonuses. If you are not already committed to engaging in regular exercise, perhaps knowing that exercise can help release residual anger will be that extra leverage you need to "just do it"!

Milder Methods

Stress Management

I include a small section here on stress management, because we know that the somatic manifestations of anger are similar if not nearly identical to those of stress. Fight or flight kicks in whether you are stressed, angry or afraid. The physiological effects are the same in any case. Knowing this, I think it is prudent to look at some ways we can work to reduce our stress.

Massage Therapy

Many of my clients and close friends have a benefits plan through their workplace, which includes between $300 and $500 per year for paramedical services (including massage therapy). It amazes me how many are aware of this service but do not take advantage of it! Massage therapy is one of the best ways I know to reduce stress and keep the physiological effects of stress from ravaging one's body.

When I began receiving massage therapy in the mid-1990's, I sneaked a peek at my chart while the therapist was out of the room. The statement that struck me most was this, "walks stiff". In fact, the muscles in my back were so knotted and tight that I walked on a tilt in order to accommodate the spasming and the pain that I experienced on a regular basis. I had become so accustomed to the pain and tension in my body that I had simply adjusted for it.

My first massage session felt like some form of ancient torture. I was certain that my entire back was black and blue. It hurt so much that I could not sit back against a chair for a couple of days. Not long after though, I found that the spring was back in my step. I learned to relax through the therapies, and eventually just fell asleep as soon as the therapist started. It was money well spent, by my benefit plan of course!

Massage therapy calms the nervous system and releases both superficial and deep muscle tension. Toxins are also released from soft tissue during massage, which is an added benefit.

Aromatherapy

It has been known for years that certain scents can stimulate pleasure, relaxation, stress, or other areas of the brain. When we were attempting to sell one of our homes, our real estate agent suggested we put on some scented oil. Guess the scent: Apple Pie!

The smell of Apple Pie reminds most people of happy days, grandmothers, Christmas dinners and all that wonderful stuff. It sends a subconscious message to the brain that this is a homey, happy environment in which to live. Neat, huh?

Aromatherapy seems to have come into its own over the last 15 to 20 years. With specialty stores, apothecaries, health food stores, and online retailers readily available, finding therapeutic grade essential oils, soaps, scented bath bombs, and the like is a fairly simple exercise.

Before you go out and start spending loads of cash on aromatherapy tools, I recommend that you do a little research, and educate yourself about which scents are most effective for stress management.

Colour Therapy

This is another area in which you may want to do a little additional research. We know that certain colours have particular meanings within society. Buddhist monks wear orange because it is perceived as a happy, peaceful colour.

I once worked in a place that was painted red. The colour red for most people is a symbol of anger. In fact, in some prisons, inmates are placed in red rooms as punishment! Can you imagine trying to hold a meeting in a red boardroom? Why do you think solitary confinement is so effective? No colour, and no light makes for a very dull existence.

I understand that some prisons are instituting pink rooms for short visits by inmates because of its calming effect. Interestingly enough, if one is left alone for too long in a pink room, the colour begins to have the opposite effect, and the individual will become more stressed. Hospitals also use muted pastels because they reduce stress and have a calming effect.

What colours do you have in your home and in your office? What do those colours mean to you? Might they be contributing to your stress on a subconscious level?

Other tools you can use

Some of the implements used to work the stiff muscles in arthritic hands are also quite effective for releasing tension from tight shoulder and neck muscles. This is due to the "ripple" effect of flexing and unflexing your hands with resistance – the muscles will become tense all the way up your arm and into your shoulder and neck. As you release the stress ball, grip strengthener, or any other such device, you will actually feel the tension flowing out of your shoulders, arms, and hands, out into the ball or device.

These types of exercises are wonderful because they can be done anywhere and very unobtrusively. Just think of the uses for these little silent partners. Driving in rush hour traffic, while attending those tense staff meetings, talking with your mother-in-law... just kidding. The joy of these little tools is that they do the job without high levels of exertion. Doing these muscle-relaxing exercises will not attract attention, nor will they disrupt anything that is going on around you.

When the Time for Confrontation Has Passed

Imagine you are at your local big box store, and a shopper runs over your foot, and then snarls at you, "Watch where you're going!" You may let it go, knowing there's no point in starting a confrontation in the store; but, what about a half-hour later, when your foot is throbbing, and all you want to do is give that mystery shopper a piece of your mind?

What about when you suddenly feel angry for no reason, and you begin to lash out at people around you? You are suddenly more irritable and easily bothered. Perhaps you begin turning your anger inward; your eating habits change, you knowingly begin to do little things that are self-destructive, but you just don't seem to care anymore.

You really don't know why you feel angry, but it's there and because there's no reason for it, you just stuff it inside and you start having physical health problems like ulcers, irritable bowel, spastic colon, insomnia, or migraines. Can these techniques we've discussed help you in situations like these?

One of my former clients had been sexually abused by her grandfather. By the time I started working with her, he had already died leaving her with scarred memories that long outlived her painful childhood. She was prone to self-abuse and would do just about anything to cause herself pain.

She obsessed about tattoos (now we call it "body art", but it still hurts to have them done). She pierced her own nose with a safety pin sterilized by the flame from her cigarette lighter. It hurt her so much that she almost lost consciousness. As soon as she could get some money together, she started getting tattoos. She had slashed her wrists several times and bore the scars to prove it.

This young woman desperately needed an outlet for her anger, but the source of her emotional pain was dead. In her mind, it was unfair for her to project her anger onto the "innocents" in her life, and of course, she must have been to blame for the abuse anyway – that's what he always told her. She deserved it. So, she directed her anger inward, abusing her body with physical mutilation and substance use, and tormenting her mind with deprecating, guilt-inducing self-talk.

Releasing her anger through alternative means wasn't just an option for my client. She had to find a way to do it or risk being unable to progress in other areas of her therapy and rehabilitation.

Along with the rehabilitative support services she received, she was also enrolled in an intensive sexual assault survivor's group that required discontinuation of her medications. The group felt that usage of medications to dampen her emotions would only hinder the healing process. She had to be able to *feel* in order to *heal*.

My role in this process was simply to help her find ways to cope with the intensity of her feelings. Anger was the most intense emotion that my client experienced. She hated the man for what he had done and resented him for dying before he received fair punishment. The angrier she became, the more she would turn on herself.

In order to break the cycle of lasting self-abuse and do it quickly, she needed an alternative. We introduced rubber bands as a way to satisfy the compulsion to induce pain by cutting her wrists. Instead of slashing, she could simply snap the band, thereby satisfying the urge without risking her life or creating fresh wounds. I encouraged her, as I had my other clients, to write in her journal so she could take more time to get in touch with her emotions as opposed to just reacting to them.

Finally, I involved her in a Gestalt exercise called 'The Empty Chair', in which she visualized her grandfather and spoke out loud all the things that she felt inside – the pain, the hurt, the loss, the guilt, and the regret. She told him how much she had loved him, and how she hated him now. She told him about her life and how it had been irrevocably changed.

Then something shifted. She began to describe to him what a strong person she was and how she had survived. He would not, could not hurt her anymore. No one would ever hurt her like that again. Somewhere in the midst of expressing her pain to a "visualized image" of her grandfather, my client experienced a pivotal shift in her consciousness. She crossed the line from "victim" to "survivor".

I would not dare say that Anger Solutions' intervention cured this girl – nor would I venture to take credit for her realization that she could move on from there. I am only grateful that I was able to contribute to her overall progress. The point of this story is that just because the person who caused you pain has died or is long gone doesn't mean that you have to be left holding the bag. Just because the time for confrontation has passed doesn't mean that you have to carry that anger with you everywhere you go. You can find a way to let the hurts of the past go if you look hard enough.

Rituals

To release emotions such unresolved grief, guilt, or anger, particularly when they are associated with those "unsolvable" problems that can cause **vicarious** trauma (trauma that occurs by listening to, seeing, or hearing about trauma experienced by another person).

Taking part in existing rituals or creating your own could be helpful in expressing and releasing the emotions associated with these events. Here are a few of examples:

- Go to a local church, light a candle for the person you lost.
- Write a poem or a letter to the person who harmed you.
- Make a "memory vault" where you can store your letter/poem/expressive writing/creative writings.

- Take something that is a poignant reminder of the situation and bury it. Hold a ceremony (e.g. speak some words over the spot where it is buried, leave a marker, send off a floating candle on a body of water, light a sky lantern) to commemorate the release of the situation and the associated emotions.

THE KEY to releasing residual anger is to find a tool or a style of release that best suits you and fits your budget. Not everyone wants a one-year membership at the gym, and not everyone can afford it! Some folks will be happy with long walks on the beach or writing letters that they can burn or dispose of later. Others may need a bit of both: a punching bag in the basement *and* a trusty journal. Make a commitment to yourself that you will at least explore the possibilities and see where they take you.

The second reminder I'd like to leave you with is to never wait until residual anger rises to a crescendo before doing something about it. It is much more sensible to be proactive rather than reactive when dealing with anger. If you know that you have some unresolved issues, it is better to work proactively to ensure that when they surface, you won't do something you'll regret later. It just makes good sense to be prepared with practical techniques you can implement right away.

Finally, remember that when in fight or flight, heart rate and blood pressure increases, and the flow of oxygen diverts from the extremities to our major organs. Often, resolving an anger-inducing issue through talking or problem solving is not enough to bring our bodies back to our base line for stress.

If we allow ourselves to remain in a state of heightened awareness, we put our bodies at risk for high blood pressure, high cholesterol, heart problems, and a multitude of other physical ailments; thus, the value of releasing residual anger.

If aggression is how you typically express anger, the chances of you changing that style completely are fairly slim. We know that one can alter the way one communicates, and that with enough leverage and motivation, one can decrease – even eliminate – harmful, aggressive behaviours. However, the urge to do something physical often remains.

If, after going through all the steps of effective anger resolution, you still feel the negative energy and stress of the situation, you may well need to do something physical to bring your base line back down to normal levels. There are other ways to effect catharsis that are suitable for a variety of emotional and behavioural types of expression: writing, participating in rituals, creating a memory vault, playing games with purpose, and releasing emotions through engaging your physiology (crying/primal screaming) are all proven methods.

After any of these exercises, particularly the physical or behavioural ones, it is paramount that you cool down just as you would after a physical workout. This is time that you can take to empty your mind of the negative thoughts, just as you have emptied your body of the negative energy of your anger. Deep breathing and allowing some time for quiet meditation will help you bring a complete balance to catharsis. The cooling down period is imperative for successfully re-attaining your baseline for stress.

Step Seven Exercises

Expressive Writing (Suggested length of activity: 10-15 min. daily)
The goal of this exercise is to help you to find meaning and resolution of the past situations or unsolvable problems that made you angry in the first place. Many types of "problems" are not easily solved using the TSA formula; it doesn't fit. Through the writing process, you may find that your emotional reactions to the trauma become more manageable and might be less disturbed by unwarranted ruminations.

Expressive writing is not a quick fix. Be aware that the benefits of expressive writing only emerge over time. In fact, as is true for any type of cathartic exercise, directly after expressing, participants typically report feeling worse and are more physiologically aroused. You should plan and prepare for some time to engage in a physical activity like walking, running, or working out after a session of expressive writing. Here are some things to consider if you decide to try this exercise.

- Write about the *emotional* aspects of an emotional event rather than the *factual* aspects.
- Remember that the goal of writing is not to find a

culprit or to punish the self. The idea is to connect to one's feelings and thoughts and write them down with the intention to express what is happening emotionally and to better understand what is going on. When feelings stay locked up, they can have detrimental effects on well-being in the long run.

- Talking about difficult emotions in an open forum (e.g. group therapy, with a therapist, or with co-workers) is challenging as this action often runs counter to the culture, making you feel embarrassed and vulnerable. Expressive writing can be a powerful way for you to "free your emotions" in a nonthreatening way.
- Take care in the storage of their writings at home. Many clients are hesitant to write for fear of others discovering and reading their journal. Feel free to dispose of your writings after you have written the day's entry. No one need ever see you have written. The process of self-expression is beneficial even if the text is immediately destroyed.
- Typically, this exercise is done in four consecutive days. However, you may wish to proceed for a longer period of time. In any case, it is important to reflect on the experience. You can do reflect privately or/and with someone you trust.
- Be careful that writing does not turn into another form of rumination. If you have not found the task helpful after three writing occasions, try something else.

Creative Writing

Much like the previous exercise, spending some time writing creatively may prove a wonderful way to express and resolve "unsolvable" problems and the emotions that accompany them.

By fictionalizing the experience, you can separate yourself from the emotional responses, assigning them to your fictional character rather than yourself. Creative writing allows you the opportunity to view and examine the problems or the anger-inducing situation through a different lens, and may prove an effective tool for gaining insight, resolution of your emotional state, and relief from the repression of those uncomfortable emotions.

Object Lesson

Here is a little exercise you can do at home to demonstrate the power of effective anger resolution.

You will need:

1. A bucket filled with water,
2. A brick or hockey puck or other heavy, sinkable object,
3. Lots of open space,
4. A mop if you're doing this indoors.

Stand 10 feet away from the bucket and try to toss the brick into the bucket. Are you successful? Not likely. If you are, I'll bet it makes a big splash. How much spillover is there? Observe the perimeter around the bucket and take note.

Now move forward approximately 1 foot. Continue trying to get the brick into the bucket from 8 feet, 7, 6, 5, even 4 feet. Is there still spillover? I'm thinking the answer is "yes". Now stand close to the bucket and drop the brick in. How easy is that? A lot less messy too, isn't it?

What do we learn from this exercise? **The bucket is you.** The water inside the bucket represents your emotions. The brick is the tool you use to resolve your emotions, and the spillover represents consequences.

Throwing the brick and trying to accurately hit your target was much more difficult at 10 feet than at close proximity. When you attempt to resolve anger from a distance, it means more work and more effort. Furthermore, the chances of making an accurate throw from 10 feet are pretty slim. Even if you hit your target, there is bound to be lots of spillover. Those emotions are going to come out in a big way, and they will affect your family, your friends, co-workers, and acquaintances, maybe even strangers if you make a big splash.

The closer you get to the bucket, the easier it becomes to accurately hit the target with the least amount of spillover. Think of this in terms of resolving anger. The closer you allow yourself to get to the source of your anger, the easier it will be to address the problem. There will be less gossip, less talking around the issue, less complaining and water cooler talk. There will be less shouting, less tension, less spillover on those who aren't involved – in effect, less mess to clean up.

Remember this the next time you feel angry with your boss, and you are tempted to tell all your co-workers and start a mutiny. Remember this when next you self-righteously refuse to assert your feelings and needs to the one who has caused you pain because, "if they don't know what they did, you won't tell them". Remember this whenever you try to reason with yourself that acting out your anger won't hurt any one except for the person involved. Then make your choice: a little confrontation, or a whole lot of frustration.

9

Step Eight: Forgive

"I think that letting go of the hatred is courageous. "It's often a lot harder to forgive than to hold a grudge."
~ *Everett Worthington*

How One Act of Forgiveness Sparked a Movement

In 2002, while writing the original manuscript for this book, I watched a portion of a television program in which a gentleman by the name of Everett Worthington told the story about how he lost his mother. He recalled that his mother was asleep in bed, when two young offenders broke into her house and began stealing its contents.

From what police could reconstruct of the crime, it appeared that the woman woke up and confronted the thieves. One of them picked up a large, blunt object and bludgeoned the poor, elderly woman to her death. When the police arrived on the scene, every item in the house with a reflecting surface had been smashed.

This man went on to tell of how he was filled with rage and hatred for the perpetrators of this heinous crime. He found that as he held on to his grief and his anger, bitterness took root in his heart, and he stopped growing. It was as though the weed of bitterness choked away whatever life he had inside and left him an angry shell of his former self. He recognized that he had to learn to forgive these youths for what they had done, or else their crime would claim yet another victim.

The turning point for him was that at which he placed himself in the shoes of the young man who killed his mother. Using the notes of the crime re-constructors, he imagined himself as a seventeen-year old boy breaking into a house with a friend for a lark. He retraced the steps of the young man, climbing through the jimmied window, wandering in the darkness around the living areas of the house, and looking for good stuff to lift.

Then, he imagined their alarm and their shock at being caught in the act by an elderly woman who was brave enough to confront them. He said that while envisioning the whole encounter, he could feel the sense of panic that that young man must have been overcome with. He could see the natural response in that intense state of fight or flight – *grab the lamp, hit the old lady before she gets to the phone and calls 9-1-1. Hit her again, just to make sure she stays unconscious until we can get away.*

He could feel the confusion and the terror of the young man as he realized he had hit her once too many and that she was soon to die. Finally, the teenager came to the knowledge that he was to blame for the death of another human being.

As he was confronted by the consequences of his actions, he looked up into a hallway mirror – and could not bear to see his own reflection for in the glass, he saw the face of a monster that had once been a boy. And so, he smashed it -- smashed everything that reflected that awful, terrible image of a boy-killer.

The minister then in tears, recounted how at that point in time – the point at which he could feel that young man's guilt and suffering for his crime – he was finally able to forgive him for killing his mother. That man, Everett Worthington, went on to establish the Campaign for Forgiveness Research through the John Templeton Foundation.

It takes a big man to do what this soft-spoken, almost bashful-looking minister did. We often have difficulty seeing things from the perspective of those we love most – can you imagine trying to see into the mind of a killer in order to forgive him?

One of my clients, a quiet, young, single mother of two small children told me something that truly struck me. She said, "I carry my anger with me everywhere. I don't want to let go of it. It has been with me so long; it is like a friend to me."

Anger was indeed her friend. It was the source from which she garnered strength to fight for what was important to her. She used her anger as her stabilizer because she did not believe that she had the strength to stand on her own without it.

The problem with making anger your friend is that like the minister who lost his mother, bitterness takes over. My client struggled in relationships, made friends with people whom she knew would take advantage of her. She allowed herself to return to abusive situations because it fed her anger. She pushed away those who would show her real love and compassion because it was easier to fend for herself than to suffer loss at their hands later on. Bitterness coloured her view of life, of love, and all those other mysteries. Although she longed to be loved and to love her children, that kind of unconditional love eluded her as long as she continued to nurture her anger.

Is a Forgiving Heart a Weak One?

The sad truth is that many of us don't want to forgive others because we think that forgiveness somehow means we condone what was done to us. People think that those who forgive are weak, and that forgiveness is a sign of "giving in".

If I forgive then I must forget; at least that is how the old saying goes. And I don't want to forget. If I forget, I leave myself open to being hurt in the same way once again.

To see the ability to forgive as a sign of weakness is to deprive oneself of a world of freedom. In all reality, it takes courage, strength, and a willing heart to forgive others. I have alluded to bitterness as an uncontrollable weed. If left untended, it will continue to grow and wind around all the chambers of one's heart until the heart finally dies for lack of room to grow. To experience true forgiveness – either as the giver or the recipient - is to find real liberation.

We all know that forgiveness is something we should do. The question most often asked is "How can I forgive that person for what they did to me?" This is a valid question; however, it is not a question that will necessarily produce the most effective answer.

The brain is a complex computer, which operates based on the programming we put into it. You also know that the process of self-evaluation is simply the process of asking questions and seeking out the answers. You can use the process of self-evaluation to help leverage yourself towards forgiveness.

Unfortunately, there is no magic pill that I could give you that will help you conjure up the will to forgive. The will to forgive can only come from within.

Take a look at these definitions according to Webster.

Forgive: (v)
To pardon
To cease to bear resentment against
To cancel (as a debt)
To exercise clemency
To grant pardon

FORGET: (v)

To lose remembrance of

To neglect inadvertently

To disregard

In one of my groups a couple was talking about how tricky this whole forgiveness thing can be. We were discussing the popular concept of "forgive and forget". The husband was saying that you can try to forgive and forget, except that whenever they get into a fight, he finds himself calling up things that his wife said or did five, ten or fifteen years ago!

I asked him why he does this. He replied, "Well, I bring those things up because I need *ammunition*." My response to him was this, "I thought you were on the same side."

What this gentleman said holds a great deal of truth. We hold on to events from the past because we need ammunition for the next fight. Why do we need ammunition to use against our partners? Think about it for one minute.

This is my theory. Nobody likes to be proven wrong in an argument. When you can't prove you're right, you lower yourself to intimidation tactics. If you can intimidate the other person, they will back away from the argument. If the other party doesn't back down, you need more leverage.

Since you already know you are wrong this time, you start digging for memories of times when *they* were wrong, and you bring it into this argument. If you succeed, the person takes the bait, and goes on the defensive.

Now you are back in control, because you have successfully diverted their attention from the issue at hand to one that died several months (maybe even years) ago.

A few problems exist with this tactic. The first problem is that the tactic often works; however, the feelings conjured up by this chain of events typically consist of more bitterness, resentment and frustration on both parties.

Each time you revive a negative or painful memory, you relive that painful memory. Calling up old transgressions inflicts new hurt on the other party, and each time you bring up something that the other party thought was resolved, you will inadvertently dwindle others' levels of trust in you.

If you say you've forgiven someone, but you bring up the old transgression every chance you get, it's hard for them to trust that you've truly let it go. Your actions will speak louder than your words.

In the early chapters of this book, you learned that belief is the basis of action. Therefore, what you believe about forgiveness will determine what you do about it. If you believe that forgiveness is for the weak and you do not want to be perceived as weak, then you will choose not to forgive others. In effect, you will be choosing to let bitterness control your heart. You will be choosing to let love die in your life. You will be choosing to stop growing.

If you believe that you will only find the closure you need through forgiveness, then you will choose to forgive. Does that mean that you will forget? Perhaps; perhaps not. Part of getting past one's past means forgetting the things that happened in the past. But we should never forget what we learned from the events of our past.

When we talk of forgiveness, often people believe that we must "cancel" the transgression and behave as though it never happened. That may work well for financial debts, but not so for emotional ones. The fact of the matter is that transgressions against one's feelings inflict much more pain than financial indiscretions or irresponsibility. Expecting people to pretend that you never hurt them is asking too much.

What we really want when we ask for forgiveness is "pardon". We want to know that the anger has dissipated, perhaps that there is some understanding, and that the individual of whom we seek forgiveness will free us from ongoing punishment.

When we talk of forgetting, what we mean is not to entirely lose remembrance of what happened. Instead, we choose to disregard what has happened to the point that it no longer pops up every time we experience negative emotions. To disregard means to not give attention to something. In other words, we choose not to look at those events of our past for the purpose of using them against others! One of my favourite sayings applies here: *Forget your past; remember only what it taught you.*

There is one common word that runs throughout all of these definitions; that word is, "choose". Forgiveness is a matter of choice. When you say that you can't forgive someone, you are really saying that you choose not to. At least be honest about it and say it like it really is. Just remember when you choose not to forgive, you are in effect choosing to choke love out of your life. The choice is yours.

Finally, as we end this chapter, I want to leave with you with a poem I wrote many years ago, as I went through the process of weeding bitterness out of my own heart. It is fitting, and I believe that based on all you now know about the anger resolution process it will resonate with you as well.

THE WEIGHT *that Besets Me*

I BEAR *your burden*
> *Heavy on my shoulders*
> *The weight suppresses my own needs.*
> *I bottle, bottle, bottle… cap*
> *For you. It is my friend*
> *Whom I despise, your burden –*
> *Yet it is a comfort to me*
> *I embrace it gladly*
> *Open arms welcome the pain.*

*Look! Look at me! I
Make myself a martyr for you,
For you. Atlas had not a
Purer purpose than I, who
Carry the weight of the world,
Shoulders sagging, knees buckling
Yet, I carry on, toting this load
For you. I bottle, bottle, bottle…
Blast!
Atlas shrugs – the burden slips
My friend is falling, falling…
It smashes against the cold, hard
Earth – breaking into pieces, splitting
Apart like an exploding melon.
Snap! Snap! I am straight again.
Some loads are not ours to carry.
I shake it off as the dust off
My shoes; walk away,
Embrace no more the tapeworm,
Which I despise. Your burden is
No longer mine to bear.*

Step Eight Exercise

Use the Dickens Pattern to create leverage in this area. Just think quickly of the ways choosing NOT to forgive has caused you pain in the past. How is being unforgiving causing you pain right now? How about in the future? If you continue not to forgive others, what do you see yourself becoming five, ten or 20 years from now?

You know that human beings will do much more to avoid pain than they will to achieve pleasure, so make your experience of unforgiveness as painful as possible. Then, do what you must to avoid the pain. Here are some questions to help you on your way.

- Why must I forgive RIGHT NOW?
- What will I gain in my relationship with this person if I forgive? What about my relationships with others?
- How might it benefit me financially to forgive?
- How will my emotions heal once I finally forgive this person?
- How will I grow spiritually if I forgive?

- How can I enhance my mental state through forgiveness?

10

Step Nine: Understand the Cyclical Nature of Anger

Anybody can become angry - that is easy. But to become angry with the right person and to the right degree and at the right time and for the right purpose, and in the right way - that is not within everybody's power and is not easy. ~ *Aristotle*

You have analyzed your anger till the cows came home. You understand that you cannot change other people, only what you expect of them. You know that you need to build on your assertiveness skills, and you are working on doing just that every day. You are looking for ways to minimize your stress and to release your residual anger, and most of all you are doing your utmost to leverage yourself towards forgiveness.

Is that all there is then? Don't be so sure. There is one more aspect of anger resolution that is integral to ensuring that it works for you. That is, understanding that anger resolution is a process or a cycle rather than a "one-shot-deal".

Let's say that you are working on a project with a team of three of your colleagues. One of your colleagues has a somewhat caustic attitude, and it is starting to grate on your nerves. After performing a bit of self-evaluation, you decide that you want to approach this individual and talk to him with the hopes of making the work environment a bit more pleasant. (You realize that he can either accept or reject what you have to say, and that you cannot make anybody change, since motivation comes from within. You are going in with eyes wide open, but still hoping for the best.)

Now, suppose that you approach this individual with a statement like the following, "_____, I have wanted to talk with you about something for a while now, but I was afraid that you might get upset with me." This kind of statement serves two purposes. First it lets the person know that you want to approach a difficult topic of conversation with him. Second, it alerts the person to the fact that you are hesitant because of the possibility of escalation.

One endearing character of most difficult people is that they like to be right. In fact, being right is almost a need. When you say that you are afraid, he may get angry, the most likely response will be… "Oh, no. I won't get angry - please talk to me about what's bothering you." Now, you have him where you want him. You see, if he has already said he won't get angry, now he has to prove it!

If your difficult person is true to form, he will do all he can to control his temper, and you will be able to express yourself. However, should he forget himself and begin to try to escalate your interaction, you may mildly respond with, "There, you see, that's what I was afraid of… you're starting to get angry." In almost every case, your difficult person will check his behaviour and discontinue the escalation.

What about when that doesn't happen? Let's be honest; some people just don't fit into any kind of mold!

We must always remember the reasons WHY we express our anger. Repeat these words: "I'm doing it for ME!" Expressing your anger is all about you. It is about making sure that you have done all you can do to release your frustration, to educate the other party, to clear the air, and to assert your wants and needs. Remember that it is not about CHANGING the other person! Motivation comes from within and the only person you can change is you. Keep this in mind as we review the cycle of anger.

Let's say you're expressing your anger and outlining your wants and needs in a particular situation. Suppose your difficult person disagrees with your perspective and says so in no uncertain terms. It is likely that your frustration signal will punch up a notch.

All you need to do is to start the process over. Think about what the other party said. What does it mean to you? How do you feel? What are you going to do about it and what might the consequences of your response be? Formulate a response and then say it. Ask for a response, all the while monitoring your body language and preparing yourself to listen. Demonstrate good listening skills and show your openness to your difficult person. Never forget that it takes two people to escalate an argument. It doesn't have to go there if you choose not to let it.

Here is how it works: you think, you say, and you ask. You listen and you respond, all the while remembering that you are doing this so that YOU can sleep better tonight.

Hey, no one said it would be easy! Moving skillfully through the anger resolution cycle is an acquired art. It takes determination, dedication, practice, and conscious effort. Your investment in acquiring this skill will pay off in endless dividends if you stick with it. That is why this book takes you step by step through the process. It is a process, and each step builds upon the skill acquired in the preceding step. As you rehearse and perfect each skill, it will eventually become part of who you are. Having to stop and think about what you should do next will occur less frequently, and you will *settle into the new, more assertive YOU.*

One Final Story

When I was a little girl, I had what you might call a very passive personality. I infrequently experimented with assertive behaviour, but honestly, I wasn't all that good at it. The youngest of three children, I learned that my opinion would be valued the least, that my side of the story would least likely be believed, and that my wants and needs were for the most part, last on the agenda.

Now, in defense of my parents and siblings, no one ever made a conscious effort to "teach" me these things, they were beliefs I formed on my own based on my experience and my own self-esteem.

As I grew older and became a pre-teen, I took on a more passive-aggressive style. I figured if my opinion had no value, I would find a way to get people to hear it without having to speak. I started writing a journal when I was in sixth grade, and I began writing short stories and poetry.

By the time I was eight years old, I had completed my first chapter book about a young girl who had no one to talk to, and lived all alone in a big, scary house. My poetry had a certain sarcastic, comedic edge to it, and I found it to be a therapeutic medium for expressing my emotions since I believed nobody wanted to listen to my voice.

Enter adolescence. I lived a secret life in my imagination, describing it in detail in my diaries. Fantasy was much more exciting than reality, so I wrote more and more - talked less and less. My mother bought me a guitar when I was a pre-teen, and I started writing songs and setting them to music. This again proved a great outlet for me, and I started sharing some of my music through song writing contests and the like.

Unfortunately, I never took it too far, again because I was the youngest and my siblings were better songwriters and

Anger Solutions

musicians than I was. Although song writing was fun, I came to believe that it was not the right outlet for me.

In my senior years of elementary school, I began to act out my emotions in full force. I took up smoking, and even experimented with recreational drugs. I started hanging out with a racier crowd and quit attending church. I stopped eating. My school-day diet basically consisted of coffee and cigarettes.

I decided that if my parents didn't believe me when I was telling them the truth, there was no point to doing so. I became a very adept storyteller. I could spin a tale like no one else, and very rarely got caught. Even when I did get caught, it was like a mad rush. I was getting attention, and even though it was negative, it felt good. I suffered frequent intense fits of anxiety, and I began to slip into a depressive state.

In high school, I got heavily involved in extra-curricular activities. Anything that meant I could stay late after school was the ticket. (That in itself is quite an amusing fact, considering that I managed to skip most of my classes without ever leaving the school grounds.) Arts, student council, drama activities, and sports were now my "drug" of choice. In fact, I even served a stint as the manager of my high school's junior boys' basketball team.

Acting proved to be a terrific outlet, and I reveled in knowing that I could do something and do it well. While acting may have been a release, I wasn't resolving much. I carried around a lot of pain, and as you know, anger turned inward can be just as destructive as anger turned outward.

I struggled with bouts of depression, evidenced mostly through my dark, despondent poetry and the subjects of my artwork. I never shared this side of myself with anyone, believing as I always did, that this was my only voice. For me, belief was truly the basis of action. Because I believed that my voice was insignificant, my self-worth continued to plummet, and I began to think that it might be better to end my life than to continue living in silence.

I count myself fortunate and credit nothing more than the grace of God, that in those moments of desperation when I reached out to others for help, the right people were in the right place, at the right time to give me the right answers.

I distinctly remember one high school friend who, after I expressed my suicidal thoughts to her, showed me her own scarred wrists and arms. I am eternally grateful to her for convincing me to focus on living instead of dying.

Not knowing how to behave assertively, but knowing I had to change; I turned the tables and began to act out more aggressively, hurting people I cared about in an attempt to reconcile my feelings of inferiority. Very quickly I realized that I could not sustain the aggressive personality - it simply isn't who I am.

It wasn't until my third year of high school that I came to the realization that my coping mechanisms were not working and that I had to work at developing a new way of living my life.

Our family moved, and with that move, I changed high schools and began to focus on academics again. Although my shift in focus was more a defense mechanism to avoid having to make new friends, it proved to be a smart move. Now immersed in my schoolwork and hanging out with friends who were emotionally stable and future focused, I found it easier to express my opinions without fear of being ridiculed.

I still used music, art, and writing as ways to express myself, but it was different now, because I had found some people who valued me for who I was. Despite these positive changes, having a healthier outlet for expressing my feelings didn't necessarily make me an emotionally healthy person.

Truth be told, I was still fairly passive in my approach to life, although I was desperately struggling to find strength to be more assertive. You see, no one ever told me what assertiveness is. I didn't even know there were different types of behaviour styles or anger styles.

I learned assertive styles of behaviour through trial and error. Even during my four years of university study in Psychology, I don't believe I utterly understood the implications of the various styles of behaviour. Inherently, I understood aggression and knew that I didn't like it. In the same vein, I appreciated and admired assertive people, but never knew on a conscious level what was the quality that I so admired.

I often wonder what my childhood would have been like had I understood what it means to act in a passive, aggressive or assertive way. Trial and error is a valuable learning tool; learning through the experience and wisdom of others is far better. Learning by trial and error is like stumbling through a well-lit room with a blindfold on, and not knowing your eyes are covered.

If you're lucky enough, someone will show kindness and help you understand that you are blindfolded and that you can take the blindfold off. Then, it's up to you to decide whether you want to continue negotiating the room with your blinders on, or if you want to remove them so you can navigate the room with ease.

I have been blessed with people who at pivotal times in my life were kind enough to say to me, "Julie, you've been blindfolded. Let me help you take those covers off your eyes and show you how easy it is to grow without them." In a way, I owe this book to them. In turn, I trust that this book will do the same for you. With the wealth of knowledge and experience that exists in the world today, there is no reason why anyone should have to learn the hard way.

It took over twenty years for me to understand my own emotions, to find a way to overcome past hurts, and to learn to truly express myself assertively. It took even longer to build a real sense of self-confidence and to understand that every voice has value and a right to be heard. Looking back, I sometimes marvel that the shy, insecure, voiceless little girl that I was evolved into an individual who could give sound counsel and deliver speeches and presentations to hundreds of people at a time.

My Challenge to You

What about you? Have you lost your voice? Do you have things you need to say, but have never found a way to say them? Perhaps you have dreams that you never imagined you could realize because your beliefs, experiences, or self-esteem do not support them.

I trust that this book has and will continue to help you discover the assertive you that lives inside. I learned some time ago, that having a goal is the first step toward accomplishing it. If you have dreams for your future, that means that somewhere deep inside of you is the belief that you can make it happen. My challenge to you is to cultivate that belief since after all; belief is the basis of action.

You may be wondering how the skill of anger resolution can help you to realize your dreams. Well, it's not as far a stretch as you may think. If you can deal with your anger in a healthy way, other emotions will be easier to express as well.

Assertiveness spills over into every area of life. Your self-esteem will rise as your successes mount. The confidence you have in your ability to express yourself doesn't just apply to anger resolution; it applies to everything! Just think of how much easier it will be to ask for what you really want, to take risks, to learn new things, and ultimately, to achieve those goals you have set for yourself!

Sometimes we make life complicated when in fact it can be quite simple. Anger Solutions is in many respects a simple concept, but it works. Will you let it work for you? Think back to when you started reading this book. What were some of the reasons you cited back then? Will you follow through on overcoming those challenges?

I trust that you will. Remember this: what you focus on is what you will achieve. Energy flows where your attention goes. If you focus on assertively expressing yourself, you will achieve it. Never give up! Godspeed; I'll be rooting for you.

Flying

*Young and sweet like coconut milk
Eyes like ackee seeds full of
Wonder. Braids trailing in the
Wind like the tail of the kite
She flies from the rooftop.
She looks up and sees the mountains
Blue, majestic blue
Cradling the valley
Pointing to the heavens
The breeze lifts, she extends the line
Up, up to the heavens
Flies the kite. She stands
On her tiptoes, as tall as
Blue, majestic blue...
Touch heaven for her.
She releases it, arms outstretched,
Spirit exultant,
Eyes like saucers watch
The kite touch heaven.*

Expand Your Feeling Word Vocabulary!

HAPPY

Merry
 Delighted
 Mirthful
 Gratified
 Exhilarated
 Joyful
 Cheerful
 Peaceful
 Gleeful
 Enraptured
 Overjoyed
 Genial
 Hilarious
 Radiant
 Congenial
 Jolly
 Spirited
 Blissful

Expand Your Feeling Word Vocabulary!

Contented
Animated
Rejoicing
Glad
Lighthearted
Satisfied
Pleased
Vivacious
Lively
Good-humoured
Jubilant
Exuberant
Elated
Excited
Playful
Hopeful
Tickled

SAD

Dismal
  Dejected
  Unhappy
  Pensive
  Depressed
  Downcast
  Sorrowful
  Melancholy
  Glum
  Gloomy
  Troubled
  Sorry
  Dispirited
  Desolate

Expand Your Feeling Word Vocabulary!

Morose
Grieved
Pessimistic
Crushed
Brokenhearted
Rueful
Heavy-hearted
Heartsick
Despondent
Anguished
Disheartened
Lamenting
Mourning
Grieving
Joyless
Bitter
Spiritless
Woebegone
Morbid
Crestfallen
Oppressed
Worried
Blighted
Hopeless

ANGRY

Stormy
   Furious
   Fierce
   Raging
   Fuming
   Enraged
   Irate

Expand Your Feeling Word Vocabulary!

Infuriated
Fiery
Enraged
Wrathful
Vexed
Indignant
Cross
Bitter
Resentful
Irritated
Sullen
Ferocious
Offended
Provoked
Hateful
Annoyed
Affronted
Displeased
Hostile
Rabid
Riled
Steamed
Provoked
Huffy
Frenzied
Exasperated
Mad
Disappointed
Troubled
Belligerent
Hostile
Contentious
Disruptive
Incensed

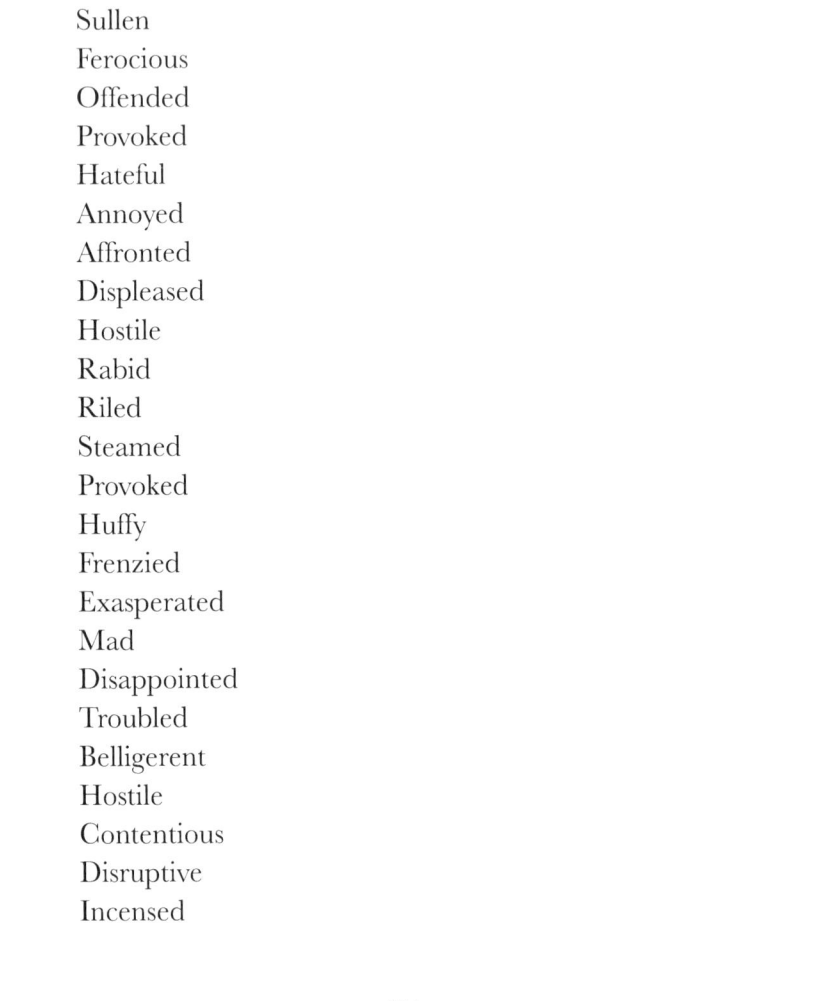

Expand Your Feeling Word Vocabulary!

AFRAID

Hesitant
- Anxious
- Disturbed
- Frightened
- Nervous
- Fearful
- Alarmed
- Discouraged
- Fidgety
- Intimidated
- Disheartened
- Perplexed
- Worried
- Perturbed
- Uneasy
- Scared
- Upset
- Terrified
- Terrorized
- Shocked
- Frozen
- Aghast
- Aroused
- Startled
- Horrified
- Petrified
- Stunned
- Rattled
- Dumb struck
- Trembling
- Jittery
- Distressed

Expand Your Feeling Word Vocabulary!

Jumpy
Leery
Shaky

References

Catharsis — www.oxfordreference.com/view/10.1093/oi/authority.20110803095555720

Dinkmeyer, and Losoncy. (1980). "Harmful Listening Skills" (adaptation), *The Encouragement Book*. Simon and Schuster.

Ekman, P. (1985). *Telling Lies*. W. W. Norton & Company; Revised Edition (Jan. 26 2009).

Ephesians 4:26, "Do not go to bed angry". *The Holy Bible*, KJV © 1973 Word Aflame Press.

Ephesians 4:15, "Speak the truth in love". *The Holy Bible*, KJV © 1973 Word Aflame Press.

Helmstetter, S. (2017). *What to Say When You Talk to Yourself.* Gallery Books.

Hoose, P. (2009). *Claudette Colvin: Twice Toward Justice*. New York: Melanie Kroupa Books.

Keyes, C., Goodman, S., Eds. (2006). *Women and Depression: A Handbook for the Social, Behavioral, and Biomedical Sciences*. Cambridge University Press.

King, M.L. (1963). *Letter from Birmingham Jail*. Retrieved from https://www.theatlantic.com/magazine/archive/2018/02/letter-from-birmingham-jail/552461/

References

Lepore, S. J., & Smyth, J. M. (Eds.). (2002). *The writing cure: How expressive writing promotes health and emotional well-being.* Washington, DC: American Psychological Association.

Mason, J. (1990). *An Enemy Called Average.* Insight International.

Mosel, S. (2021). *Depression, Anger, and Addiction: The Role of Emotions in Recovery and Treatment.* American Addiction Centers. Retrieved from https://www.americanaddictioncenters.org/co-occuring-disorders/emotions-in-recovery-and-treatment.

Peele, S. (1982). The Human Side of Addiction: What Caused John Belushi's Death? *US Journal of Drug and Alcohol Dependence,* April 1982. Retrieved from https://www.peele.net/lib/belushi.html.

Pennebaker, J. W. (1997). *Opening up: The healing power of expressing emotions.* New York: Guilford Press.

Pennebaker, J. W. (1999). *Health effects of expressing emotions through writing.* Biofeedback, 27, 6–9, 14.

Pennebaker, J. W. (2004). *Writing to heal: A guided journal for recovering from trauma and emotional upheaval.* Oakland, CA: New Harbinger Press.

Robbins, A. (1996). *Personal Power II.* Nightingale Conant.

Taylor, S., Cousino Klein, L., Lewis, B., Gruenewald, T., Gurung, R., and Updegraff, J. (2000). Behavioral responses to Stress in Females: Tend and Befriend, Not Fight or Flight. *Psychological Review,* 107:3, 411-429.

Verma, R., Balhara, Y., Gupta, C. (2011). Gender Differences in Stress Response: Role of Developmental and Biological Determinants. Industrial Psychiatry Journal, Vol. 20:1, 4-10.

Worthington, Everett L, Jr. (2019). A Campaign for Forgiveness Research: Lessons in Studying a Virtue. *Journal of Psychology and Christianity*, suppl. Special Issue: Interdisciplinary Collaboration; Batavia Vol. 38, Iss. 3:184-190.

Also by Julie A Christiansen

Anger Solutions™ Facilitators Manual

For counsellors and helping professionals to implement the Anger Solutions™ model of anger resolution with individuals or groups.

Anger Solutions™ "Releasing Residual Anger" Audio Program

Includes an overview and review of the basic principles of the Anger Solutions™ method of anger resolution, along with a detailed, step-by-step visualization of the "Empty Chair" exercise. Relaxation and breathing techniques included as well.

Anger Solutions by the Book: Biblical Principles for Resolving Anger (with Companion Workbook)

Anger Solutions for Youth Facilitator Guide and Participant Workbook

Designed for group sessions with youth at risk, youth justice programs or for general youth population aged 13 to 17.

When the Last Straw Falls: 30 Ways to Keep Stress from Breaking Your Back

Getting Past Your Past

An audio program available on CD with Workbook

Top Ten Lists to Live By

A motivational book of lists to help you become more assertive, resolve anger, make important decisions wisely, and to cope with life's challenges. Available for purchase from www.buybooksontheweb.com.

Visit Julie's website at: www.angersolution.com

Bullying is Not a Game: A Parents' Survival Guide

By Julie Christiansen and Laurie Flasko

About the Author

Julie Christiansen, MA, is an award-winning international public speaker, author, and psychotherapist. Julie developed the Anger Solutions method of anger resolution, and has authored several books about anger, stress, bullying and coping with crisis. She has a deep love for the written word, and she is passionate about helping to leverage people into radical, positive, lasting change through her work.

Known as "The Anger Lady", She has appeared as an expert for various print, radio, and television media outlets. She has also consulted with various producers providing insight into their program content – including the *Anderson Cooper Show*, *The Hunted*, and *Investigations Discovery*.

Julie is a two-time nominee finalist for the YWCA Women of Distinction Awards; she was the recipient of Niagara's 40 Under 40 Award, and in 2015 received the Toastmasters Communication & Leadership Award. Her work in Anger Solutions coupled with her work in academia landed her on the list of the 40 Most Influential Forensic Psychologists.

Julie has been married to her soul mate Stevan for more than 30 years. They reside in the Niagara Region of Ontario, Canada with two of their three children and their toy poodle, Forrest Gump.

Anger Solutions has been reviewed by a Clinical Psychologist, a Neuropsychologist, as well as a Doctor of Metaphysical Science, and is recognized by the Centre for Excellence in Children's Mental Health as evidence-based. Since we began documenting program outcomes in 2003, Anger Solutions continues to boast an exemplary success rate; that is to say, a minimum of 80% of group and individual participants go on to apply their acquired skills and report a marked improvement in their quality of life as a direct result of this program.

Booking

Julie is available to deliver conference keynotes, workshops, training seminars, for your next event. To request Julie for an upcoming event, please visit the marketplace at www.espeakers.com.

Coaching

Coaching is quickly becoming one of the leading tools that successful people use to live extraordinary lives. Through weekly coaching sessions, clients identify what is most important to them and learn to align their thoughts, words, and behaviours accordingly. Coaching is proven to work when two factors are present: the client is willing to learn, grow, and take action; and there is a gap between where clients are and where they want to be. Even Tiger Woods has a coach! To learn more about the Anger Solutions Coaching Model and how it can help you, contact Julie via: www.juliechristiansen.com.

Web Presence and Social Media

www.angersolution.com
www.leverageu.ca
www.juliechristiansen.com

Instagram:
@julz_christiansen
@leverage_u

Twitter:
@theangerlady

LinkedIn:
https://www.linkedin.com/in/juliechristiansen/

Anger Solutions Success Stories

What People Are Saying About Anger Solutions™

"Julie's teachings helped me to be able to pull out the good in everyone around me. It was easy to receive what she had to say without the feeling of rejection or the feeling that everything is my fault. I came out of the course a strong, more confident person."
~ Cindy G., Anger Solutions™ participant

"Not only have I benefited from this, I will pass this knowledge on to my family and friends in the future."
~ Steve P., Anger Solutions™ participant

"I have learned to evaluate my choice of behaviour and to make better decisions of how I will respond to those frustrating and difficult times. I have noticed I have become more assertive in and outside of the home. I have grown in self-esteem and confidence."
Sophia C., Anger Solutions™ participant

"I wish I could have found you 20 years ago. My life would have been totally different. My kids' lives would have been different. (My daughter) is picking up my new anger solution skills. She will not have to live the way I have! Thank you!"
Anger Solutions™ Coaching client – Ontario

"Thank you so much for helping me on both a professional and personal level. You were there for me when I most needed it. Thank you, Julie."
Jordan S.~ Coaching client – Ontario

"You are like Oprah for the office."
K. Hale – Degersheim, Switzerland

Notes

Manufactured by Amazon.ca
Bolton, ON